The Dead Sea Scrolls
and the
Originality of Christ

The Dead Sea Scrolls

and the

Originality of Christ

by GEOFFREY GRAYSTONE

Sheed & Ward • New York

AUTHOR'S FOREWORD

These brief chapters on one aspect of the Dead Sea Scrolls appeared originally as articles in the *Irish Theological Quarterly* under the title, "The Dead Sea Scrolls and the New Testament." It is in the hope that they may be of interest to a wider public that they are now reproduced in book form, thanks to the initiative and kind co-operation of Messrs. Sheed and Ward, Inc.

The author's acknowledgments are also due to the Revd. Editors of the *Irish Theological Quarterly*, and to Messrs. Desclée and the Revd. G. Vermès, for permission to use material contained in *Les Manuscrits du Désert de Juda* (2nd ed., 1954).

Rome, 30th January, 1956.

The Dead Sea Scrolls
and the
Originality of Christ

CHAPTER ONE

It is now some seven years since the first intimation was given of the discovery of ancient Hebrew manuscripts in a cave in the Desert of Judea. Since then a very extensive literature has grown up around these "Dead Sea Scrolls," as they are popularly, though perhaps inaccurately, referred to.[1] Further discoveries, fast succeeding one another, together with the gradual publication of the various manuscripts and fragments, and the systematic excavation of the localities concerned, have all tended to emphasize the fact that much of what has been written was a little premature. Even at present, when a great quantity of fragmentary texts remains to be published, and when the possibility of fresh finds can by no means be ruled out, whatever is written must still be of a somewhat provisional character.

The Dead Sea Scrolls have shed light on a number of

3

questions—archaeology, palaeography, the text of the Old Testament, Jewish history, and so on. However, what I am specifically concerned with here is a matter of possibly more general interest, namely, the connexion of the newly-found documents with the New Testament, or, if you will, the possible relationship of the people or sect who produced these documents with the origins, the spread, the organization and tenets of Christianity. It is well known that a number of theories and opinions, one or two a little advanced, have been ventilated on this question. M. Dupont-Sommer, Professor of the Sorbonne, in a work that evoked no little controversy when it was first published in 1950, suggested that it was "from the womb of this spiritual ferment [i.e. the Essenian movement which, he believed, produced the scrolls] that Christianity emerged."[2] So distinguished an Orientalist as the American Professor Dr. Albright was of opinion that the new knowledge derived from the Scrolls "bids fair to revolutionize our approach to the beginnings of Christianity."[3] Professor Rowley of Manchester University, in the course of a recent broadcast talk, expressed himself with more reserve: "That the sect of the scrolls was a far less dynamic group than the Church of the New Testament is certain; but its expressions and ideas appear to have been taken up and invested with a new meaning."[4] In fact, it has been suggested that the Jewish background of the Gospels and of the New

4

Testament generally must be sought, not in the rabbinical writings with their Pharisaic tradition—as was done by Strack and Billerbeck in their well-known commentary —but in the writings and beliefs of the sect of Qumran.[5] No less than five hundred parallels between the New Testament and the scrolls have been cited in the course of systematic comparisons instituted by two Continental scholars.[6] What is the significance of these points of contact and how much do they prove?

THE STORY OF THE SCROLLS

In order to attempt an answer to this question, some account, however brief, must first be given of the discovery and nature of the documents in question, and especially of the identity, origins, organization, practices and tenets of the people responsible for them.[7]

It was in a cave to the west of the Dead Sea, near certain ruins known as Khirbet Qumran, that the Bedouin discovered the first manuscripts in 1947. They were scrolls, more or less complete, carefully wrapped in linen and preserved in jars. They comprised biblical texts in Hebrew—two scrolls of Isaias, one complete, the other incomplete; writings hitherto unknown, which were quickly labelled "Sectarian"—a Commentary or "Midrash" on the first two chapters of Habacuc, the "War of the Sons of Light and the Sons of Darkness," a collection of thirty-five hymns or "Thanksgiving Songs," and the Community Rule or "Manual of Discipline"; finally, a work of an apocalyptic character, apparently the lost "Apocalypse of Lamech." All these manuscripts, originally divided between two principal owners, have now been published in full, with the exception of the last-named, which has not yet been unrolled on account of its fragile condition.[8] In addition, a large quantity of fragments, some six hundred in number—either purchased from the Bedouin and from dealers, or collected during the systematic excavation of the cave in 1949—came into the possession of the Palestine Museum, and were published last year in a single volume.[9]

The genuineness of these scrolls, hotly contested at first in certain quarters, is now generally accepted, following the rediscovery of the cave and its systematic excavation in 1949. Discussion as to the problem of their precise age lasted somewhat longer—whether we speak of the date of the original composition of the works in question, or the date the actual scrolls were copied, or the date of their deposit in the cave; these are distinct, though related questions. Internal evidence could not by itself settle the first question, nor could palaeography supply a certain answer to the second.[10] To the third question, the date of the deposit, the *terminus ad quem* for the dating of the scrolls, archaeology was able to give a solution that is now pretty generally accepted. The adjacent ruins of Qumran—the nearest site inhabited in antiquity—were carefully explored under the direction of the Department of Antiquities of the Kingdom of Jordan, and of the Ecole Biblique of Jerusalem, first at the end of 1951, and then in three further seasons' work till 1955.[11] In the first season's work, a complete jar, of exactly the same type as those used to store the scrolls in the cave, together with fragments of lamps and cooking utensils also corresponding to those discovered in the cave, were found in association with coins dating from the time of Augustus to that of the Jewish Revolt of A.D. 66-70. During this latter period, so the evidence indicated, the buildings were destroyed by fire and abandoned. The conclusion was fairly drawn that the scrolls were stored away for safe-keeping before A.D. 70, and thus belonged to the early New Testament or pre-Christian period.[12]

THE COMMUNITY OF QUMRAN

Subsequent excavation of the site, together with systematic exploration of the whole adjoining area in March 1952,[13] served to confirm these conclusions and to shed light on the community or sect—for such it was —that was responsible for the manuscripts. The central building—distinguished by large rooms which emphasized its community character—was built during the reign of the Hasmonean John Hyrcanus (135-104 B.C.) and occupied till about 30 B.C., when it was ruined by an earthquake. It was rebuilt early in the first century A.D. by the same community and occupied till the time of the First Jewish War. It was not exactly a monastery as we understand it, but a community centre, a place where the sectaries gathered for assemblies, common meals and work of various kinds. The individuals seemed to have lived in caves and tents in the vicinity.[14] The whole enclosure was walled, with a tower for defence, there was a large hall for reunions, a kitchen and several cisterns—which served not simply for water-supply (holding water brought by aqueduct from the Wadi), but also for the various ritual purifications mentioned in the documents. In the level of the building restored in the first century A.D. were found the remains of a large room evidently used as a "scriptorium." Here was a long low table equipped with inkwells, benches and basins (apparently for ritual purification before writing). There was even a piece of potsherd inscribed with the letters of the Hebrew alphabet. One might reasonably suppose that writing and reading were taught and practised here, and that here too many of the

8

scrolls were copied. In an area excavated to the south and west of the main building were found the community mill, oven and storage bins, and an extensive and well-preserved establishment for the manufacture of pottery of every description. Ample evidence points to the destruction of the buildings by act of war, apparently by the troops of Titus, who were known to be in this area prior to the final assault on the Holy City. Finally, after the Community had fled, taking their valuables with them, the site was temporarily occupied—with the construction of some small rooms—as a Roman outpost, and, after an interval, as a centre of resistance by the Jewish insurgents in the abortive revolt of Bar Kokhba in A.D. 132-135.

Between the building and the shores of the Dead Sea was the community cemetery, with its thousand-odd tombs. In striking contrast with Jewish tombs around Jerusalem of the same period, the graves of Qumran are marked with every token of austerity and simplicity: the bodies are simply laid in the earth, with a simple cairn of stones above, without coffin, grave-apparel or offerings.

In the adjoining region, explored in March 1952, various caves and rock-fissures, up to forty in number, were examined and found to have been used for storage and temporary human occupation. Fragments of manuscripts were found in two of them (referred to as 2Q

9

and 3Q).[15] Subsequent investigations by the Bedouin led to the discovery of a fourth hiding-place (4Q), artificially constructed on the edge of the plateau which houses the buildings of Qumran. This was systematically excavated in September 1952, and was found to have been originally the richest of all in manuscript content, though now only fragmentary texts remained. Only one or two of these have been published, but they are known to include a considerable body of "Sectarian" texts, some known already and many unknown. At the same time fragments of scrolls were unearthed in two further caves (5Q and 6Q). The community library, and hence the literary output of the community, must have been very considerable: the first cave is estimated to have contained originally some seventy manuscripts, and the fourth at least a hundred. These caves—apart from the influence of natural destructive forces—have clearly been despoiled by human hands at different points in history: in fact there is more than one record of such apparent despoliation in antiquity.[16]

THE DAMASCUS DOCUMENT AND THE ESSENES

What was this community—which certainly numbered several hundred—and which wrote so much? Soon after

10

the first Sectarian scrolls were, published, striking resemblances were noted between them and a somewhat
enigmatic document, discovered, in two medieval copies,
in the *Genizah,* or store-place for disused manuscripts,
of a synagogue in Cairo, in the year 1896. This was
known as the "Sadokite Document" (from its many
allusions to the "sons of Sadoq") or the Damascus Document (because it speaks of a sect that fled to Damascus
and lived there under a "new covenant").[17] It was a kind
of description and rule-book of an exclusive Jewish sect,
originating in the second century B.C. according to the
chronological indications given, which broke away from
official Judaism under the inspiration of priests and
levites, who, under their chosen title "sons of Sadoq,"
claimed pure and lawful descent from the High Priest of
that name in the time of David. Their principal or-
ganizer was a certain "Teacher of Righteousness," who,
bitterly opposed by his adversary, the "Wicked Priest"
or "Man of Lying," was persecuted and fled in exile to
Damascus, where he gathered his disciples around him.
They bound themselves there by a "New Alliance,"
living in common under a strict rule, regarding themselves as the true "remnant of Israel," fervently attached
to the Law and living in expectation of the proximate
advent of the Messiah of Aaron and Israel and of the
Day of Judgment.[18]

In the Qumran scrolls, the same mysterious personages—the Teacher of Righteousness and his adversaries —are met with, notably in the Habacuc Midrash. The Community Rule presents many striking points of contact with the Damascus Document: the "Alliance," the "sons of Sadoq," Messiah of Aaron and Israel, mention of the "Book of Hagu" prescribed for meditation in the Damascus Writing, and many details of rule and organization. Moreover, a fragment of this Damascus Document was found in the fourth cave of Qumran. Evidence of the relationship between the Qumran scrolls and the Damascus Document is, writes Professor Rowley, "overwhelming."[19]

There are, however, certain differences discernible: e.g., the Damascus sectaries permitted marriage, whilst those of Qumran were apparently celibate; community of property was not as absolute with the former as with the latter. These differences have led some to think of the Damascus Document and the Qumran Rule as representing two distinct sects of one common federation, or, more probably, one and the same sect at different stages of its history.[20] However, we cannot yet speak with certainty, because additional fragments of the Qumran Rule, including an earlier form, have yet to be published.

Moreover, it was also pointed out from the first that the Qumran sect was akin to the obscure Jewish sect

12

of the Essenes, which existed in New Testament times. Though not mentioned in the New Testament, they are known to us from the description of the Jewish historian Josephus, and from references of Philo of Alexandria, Pliny the Elder, Dio Chrysostomos and some of the early Christian Fathers, notably St. Jerome.[21] The beliefs and practices of this sect are very like those of the Qumran community, e.g., exclusiveness, practice of celibacy and community of goods, great attention to ritual purity, scrutiny of the Law, secret doctrines and practices, abundant literary activity, allegorical exegesis of the Old Testament, general organization, etc. The location of Khirbet Qumran corresponds exactly to the location of the principal centre of the Essenes as given by Pliny: near the western shores of the Dead Sea, yet far enough away not to be molested by noisome exhalations, and with the city of Engaddi to the south.[22] Yet here again there are slight differences, e.g., according to Josephus, the Essenes were found scattered through the villages of Palestine and Syria; they opposed slavery, and practised almsgiving and a measure of hospitality— points not mentioned in the Qumran rule. It has been suggested, then, that the first-century Essenes represent a third stage of which the Damascus sectaries and those of Qumran were the first and second respectively. At all events, it is more correct to speak of the Qumran community as a group of Essenes. "It is therefore very probable," writes Père de Vaux, "that the Khirbet represents the conventual building of a group, possibly the principal group, of Essenians."[23]

ORIGINS OF THE QUMRAN SECT

Regarding the precise origins of the Qumran sect, and notably the historical identification of the persons mentioned in their scrolls (Teacher of Righteousness, Wicked Priest, the invading Kittim, etc.), there has been a wealth of divergent theories.[24] However, there is some measure of agreement now among scholars as regards the broad outlines of the genesis and history of the sect. Here is how the Dominican Fathers actually working on the Cave material in Jerusalem would put it. The remote origins of the sect take us back to the pietist milieu centred around the Temple of Jerusalem early in the second century B.C. The sect emerged as a distinct body in the Machabean revolt of 166 B.C., as an element in the *Hasidim* (the "pious"), who rallied to the standard of Judas. From this period dates the War Scroll, and possibly an early form of the Rule. After some years (twenty is the figure given in the Damascus Document), the sect definitely broke with official Judaism. This was probably in the time of the early Hasmoneans (after 134 B.C.), though others would date it to the reigns of the two Machabees, Jonathan (160-142) and Simon (142-134). Then the sect was led into "exile," in all probability, by the Teacher of Righteousness, who organized it there. "Damascus," as Père de Vaux points out, is almost certainly a symbolic name for Qumran. From the second period date the Hymns, some, if not all, of which were composed by the Teacher of Righteousness, the Habacuc Commentary and the gradual compilation of the Rule, of which the same Teacher was responsible for certain sections and probably for the final compilation of the whole.[25]

A final point regarding the connexions of the Qumran sect. Many points of contact exist between their writings and the Old Testament Apocrypha (the books of Henoch and of Jubilees, the Testament of the Twelve Patriarchs, the Assumption of Moses etc.), which date from the second century B.C. to the first century A.D. It is significant that in nearly all the Qumran caves fragments of these apocrypha, and of other similar works previously unknown or lost, have been found. The evidence seems to point more and more to the conclusion that it was the Qumran community—or, at all events, the general movement of which it was a part—that was responsible for these writings.

"To live according to the rule of the community, to seek God . . . to practise what is good and just in his sight, in conformity with what he ordained through Moses and through all his prophets, his servants, to love all that he has chosen and to hate all that he has rejected, withdrawing oneself from evil and adhering to every good work; to practise truth, justice and right on the earth; no longer to walk in the obstinacy of a guilty heart, by following the attractions of impurity and doing every evil; to bring those who are willing to practise the precepts of God in the alliance of grace, according to God's plan; to comport themselves as men that are perfect before him, according to all that has been revealed to their solemn assemblies; to love the Children of Light, each according to his allotted position in God's plans, and to hate all the Children of Darkness, each one according to his guilt in according with God's vengeance."[26]

Thus begins the Community Rule, and in these words we are told a good deal about its purpose and spirit. Far from being a mere pious association, the sect of Qumran had all the features of a monastic order, with a definite aim, a distinct organization and hierarchy, and customs

16

and beliefs that marked it off from the main body of Judaism, from which it was effectively separated. It was an "Israel within Israel," or better, *the* only true Israel, the faithful "remnant" of the latter days which the prophets foretold. Those who joined pledged themselves to "seek God," according to the Law of Moses and the Prophets, and the special revelations granted to the sect. They were to practise all virtues in common, as "children of light" cut off from the society of "children of darkness," men of untruth and iniquity. Living thus in constant study of the Law and of their own "revealed" interpretations of it, they awaited the advent of the days of the Messiah and of God's judgment, at which they were to assist.

As an "Israel in miniature," the Qumran Community was made up of priests and laymen, "Aaron and Israel," organized in groups or "camps" of thousands, hundreds, fifties and tens—though it is not necessary to take these figures literally. Each one had his allotted place, from which he must not depart. Priests, "sons of Sadoq," take precedence in the government of the Community; in all probability, the *Mebaqqer*, Overseer or Inspector, who was over the whole Community, was himself a priest.[27] However, the direction of Community affairs was also in the hands of the council of the "Great" over which he presided. The "Great" were simply fully-fledged

17

members. They met for deliberations of all kinds: to admit new members, to judge and impose penalties, to excommunicate and re-admit. Absolute obedience was insisted on in the Community; flagrant revolt involved dismissal, simple disobedience spelt exclusion from community practices for a certain period of time.

He who entered the Community made a complete oblation of himself, of all his talents and all his possessions: "they will bring with them all their learning, all their faculties and all their possessions into the Community of God, in order to purify their learning by the truth of the precepts of God, to regulate the use of their faculties according to the perfection of his ways and their possessions according to the plan of his righteousness."[28] Insistence was laid on the practice of the virtues, charity, humility and docility. Among Community practices, one of the most important was the solemn repast or ritual banquet, beginning with the priest's blessing over the "bread and must [unfermented wine]." Prayer in common, at daybreak and sundown, was a point of rule, as also the vigil for the third part of the night, spent in "reading of the Book [i.e. Scripture], in the pursuit of justice [i.e. study of the Law], and in the common blessing [i.e. prayer]."[29] One man in ten was released from all other duties in order to search the Law "day and night," in order to discover the "hidden things" contained in it and make them known to his confrères. So highly was prayer esteemed, that the "offering of the lips" was held to be of greater value than the "fat of sacrifices," and perfect conduct of more worth than ritual offerings. Sacrifices in the Temple were not, apparently, rejected, but at least they were relegated to second place.[30]

Another practice of great importance was the Community reunions: the proceedings were most carefully regulated—each must take his place in exact order of precedence, order must reign over the discussions and there must be nothing unseemly. Insistence on purity was emphasized by the frequent ritual baths and ablutions. It seems highly probable that celibacy was the rule, though this is not absolutely certain.[31]

Community of property was the rule—each must hand over his property and salary, where this existed, to the "treasurer." There was to be no mingling of one's possessions with the impure goods of outsiders. Nothing was to be accepted from outsiders, save what was bought for money. Great care of common property was enjoined.[32] We are told little of the daily work of the sectaries, though Josephus says of the Essenes that they practised manual work during much of the day. Though today the desert of Judea is barren, it may well be that, by dint of careful irrigation and of measures to prevent soil-erosion, stock-raising and even a little cultivation was possible for the community. The making of pottery, and work in the scriptorium—not only writing, but preparing the animal skins of which the scrolls were made—together with weaving and tent-making, would be other occupations.

The stages of initiation into the Community were as follows. The candidate was first examined by the *Mebaqqer*, and, if suitable, he publicly bound himself by oath "to be converted to the Law of Moses . . . in accordance with all that has been revealed to the sons of Sadoq, the priests . . . and to the Great Assembly of the men of their Alliance."[33] In the same public ceremony of admission, the candidate confessed his sins, and the priests and levites recited the blessings and curses attached to the Law of Moses. The whole ceremony was thus a real "conversion," though the candidate was not immediately admitted to the assembly of the "Great." He passed through a period of postulancy, the duration of which is not stated; this was a time of instruction and purification, though the postulant was excluded from most of the common observances. After a favourable vote on the part of the Assembly, there began a novitiate of two years. In the first year, instruction continued, and the novice joined in certain common practices, not, however, the ritual purifications; he retained his property, which was still regarded as "impure." In the second year—if the vote was again favourable—he might take part in the purifications, and his goods were handed over to the treasurer, who kept them in reserve; he was still barred from the ritual meal and, of course, the assembly. After two years and a final scrutiny, he was definitely admitted to full community status (without special ceremony): he took his place among the "Great" in his allotted position, his goods were incorporated into the community assets, he was admitted to assemblies and the solemn meals.[34] However, total fidelity to the Law and the rules of the Community was required of him. A lengthy penal code lists faults with their corresponding penalties, varying from full excommunication (e.g. for pronouncing the sacred name Yahweh, for flagrant breach of the Law) to exclusions from common acts for a longer or shorter period (e.g., for indeliberate faults against the Law, for fraud, outburst of anger, lesser disobedience, etc.).

DOCTRINES OF THE COMMUNITY

The religious outlook of the Community was based on a deep attachment to the Mosaic Law and whole-hearted obedience to its prescriptions. The Damascus Document distinguishes five periods of sacred history. In the first three of these, from the beginnings till the founding of the Sect, few were found completely faithful, viz., Noe, Abraham, Isaac, Jacob, Moses and Sadoq. With the first "penitents" who laid the foundations of the sect, began the fourth period and a "return to the Law of Moses." The fifth and last period began with the preaching and work of the Teacher of Righteousness: he it was who renewed the Sinaitic Covenant in a "New Alliance" to which all who were willing to follow his guidance bound themselves by oath.[35]

Hence the great insistence of the sectaries on purity—not merely external, but such as involved also complete conversion of heart. Hence, too, their utter separation, not only from the Gentiles, but even from their fellow-Jews (not so generous as they), even from the Temple and its worship. Hence, too, in all probability, their renunciation of marriage. The Law must be fully observed, and—here is the capital point—it could only be so observed in the Community.

For, in truth, the Community of Qumran was an assembly of the predestined. In every age of sacred history God had preserved a faithful "remnant" of "elect"—the Patriarchs, Moses, Sadoq, the first "penitents." In the present age, it was they, faithful "sons of

22

Sadoq," who were God's elect, who had escaped God's chastisement meted out even on earth to the men of lying and iniquity. Yet, elect as they were, their standing demanded a voluntary engagement on their part, as we saw above in regard to entry into the Community. Physical descent from Abraham and circumcision were not enough for salvation.

Yet God's special call and choice of them, which made them "children of grace," was duly emphasized. Hence, in the Thanksgiving Songs, they enlarge on man's weakness and nothingness—he is as "clay in the hands of the potter"—and extol the majesty and activity of God, who alone creates, bestows justice, teaches wisdom and strengthens to keep his Law and endure persecution.

Who were their teachers? Moses, of course, was all-important, and so, to some extent, Sadoq. More immediately, it was the Teacher of Righteousness. Faith in his mission and fidelity to his message were essential. He had received special "revelations" for a full understanding of the Law and Prophets; and after him, others, too, among the "Great" had been similarly enlightened.

We come now to a basic theological tenet of the sect, one for which most parallels from the New Testament and elsewhere have been cited.[36] This is the instruction on the "Two Ways" or "Two Spirits," found in the Rule, III, 13-IV. The salvific order, according to the sect, is based on absolute divine predestination *ante praevisa merita et demerita:* "From the God of knowledge proceeds all that is and all that will be, and before ever they exist, God has already determined their destiny. Existing according to their several norms, in conformity with his glorious plan, without affecting any change in it, they will engage on their activity . . . He it is who created man for the domination of the world, and has placed before him the two spirits, so that he may be led by them even till the time of the visitation: these are the spirits of truth and of iniquity."[37] What are these "two spirits"? It seems we should regard them as two spiritual currents or tendencies, rather than as definite beings or entities.

None the less, those who are led by either spirit come under the influence and rulership of two opposed powers: the Prince of Light (Angel of Truth), and the Angel of Darkness (*Belial* or *Mastema*). According as men follow the one or the other, they are "sons of light" and "sons of justice," or "sons of darkness" and "sons of iniquity." "In the hands of the Prince of Light is the government of the sons of justice; they shall walk in the paths of light . . . in the hands of the Angel of Darkness is the government of the sons of iniquity; they shall walk in the paths of darkness."[38]

24

These two paths are radically opposed, and implacable hostility exists between those who follow them; nay more, the sons of justice will suffer persecution at the hands of the sons of iniquity, "for God has placed the two spirits in equal proportion until the appointed time and the great renewal . . . till then the spirits of truth and iniquity will contend for the hearts of men."[39] God has set a term to this great moral struggle: then, the sons of light will be rewarded with eternal life,[40] the sons of darkness will be consigned to the Pit, to endless shame, to destruction in the fires of darkness.

So it was that the faithful sons of light must needs separate themselves in a community from fellowship with the sons of darkness, and there live as God's "elect," his "saints," awaiting the time of God's intervention, which would be heralded by the advent of the Messiah. Or rather, they expected two Messiahs, one of Aaron, the other of Israel, corresponding to the twofold aspect of the Community. Messianic expectation was certainly intense, though we are not told a great deal about the work and role of the two anointed ones. They would come in times of judgment and salvation, to teach justice; they are spoken of as the Priest-in-Chief and the Prince respectively; they would organize the Messianic banquet.[41]

It is clear that, on many points, the Community of Qumran went beyond the beliefs and practices of contemporary Judaism. In what relation did it stand to Christianity?

First, a few general points. It is clear that the Qumran community was a closed sect, a sect of initiates, with their own jealously-guarded practices, beliefs and writings. They did not encourage contact with outsiders, save where strictly necessary. Hence I think we should be slow to admit, simply on the score of verbal likenesses, contacts between them and the early Christian Church, at least before the year 70 A.D.

Secondly, to come to fundamentals, the Qumran sect was based essentially on the Mosaic Law, it was contained within the framework of the Sinaitic Covenant, even though it claimed fuller lights for understanding its extent and obligations. The Christian faith was based on the belief that the Death of Christ had abrogated the Sinaitic Covenant and terminated the régime of the Mosaic Law. In one of his earliest epistles, St. Paul likens the era of the Law to the time of childhood, when the son is little better than a slave in his Father's house (Gal. 4:1-3). Then God sent his Son to redeem us from the Law and make us his sons and heirs: "When the fullness of time was come, God sent his Son, made of a woman, made under the Law; that he might redeem them who were under the Law; that we might receive the adoption of sons" (Gal. 4:4-5). Texts of this kind could be multiplied.

It follows that the Qumran sect was essentially forward-looking, expecting the advent of a Messiah yet to come. Christianity recognised that he had already come, that God had sent his Son to redeem men.

The Qumran sect was rigidly exclusive—for Jews alone, and then only for those Jews who were eternally called and elected, and who bound themselves under the New Alliance to all the rules of the Sect. The others were "outside the pale" and should be "hated" as being the object of God's vengeance. The Christian faith, need we say it, embraced all men, Jew and Gentile; it was preached to all, and all who were willing to believe and be baptized might enter the fold. The central "mystery" of the Faith, as expounded by St. Paul in the Epistles of the Captivity (Ephesians and Colossians particularly) concerned God's eternal plan to call all men, Gentiles as well as Jews, into the one Mystical Body of Christ who had redeemed them.

We might speak too of such fundamental doctrines—unknown to the sect—as the Blessed Trinity, the Divinity and Redemptive Death of Christ—but enough has been said for the moment to underline the fundamental differences that existed between the Qumran Sect and the Church of the New Law. The latter did not "emerge from the womb of the spiritual ferment" of which the Qumran community was part. The early Christians were well enough aware of the unique origin of their religion; its source lay neither in Judaism nor in Hellenism, but in the Person, preaching and redemptive work of the Son of God Incarnate. St. Paul sums up the matter well, speaking of the basic Christian doctrine of the Redemptive Death of Christ: "We preach Christ crucified; unto the Jews indeed a stumbling-block, and unto the Gentiles foolishness . . ." (1 Cor. 1:23).

Approaching the matter from another angle, it is significant, as Canon Coppens has pointed out,[42] that the documents of Qumran offer more abundant points of contact with the apostolic preaching and the later New Testament writings (Acts, to some extent, the Captivity Epistles and the Joannine writings) than with the primitive gospel catechesis (fewer contacts in Matthew and Luke, fewer still in Mark and the earlier Pauline epistles to the Churches). Influence, then, on the origins of Christianity, could only be slight and negligible. Similarly, the Qumran scrolls offer few points of contact with fundamental Christian doctrines, though more with doctrines that are relatively secondary (e.g. angelology), and more with matters of moral teaching and organization, especially in points that arose only during the apostolic age.

If Christianity did not in any sense owe its origins to the Qumran sect, may we say that it owed something to it by way of borrowed terminology and ideas, granted that these expressions and ideas were invested with new or fuller meaning? What conclusion is to be drawn from those resemblances in organization (e.g. community of goods), in names and titles (e.g. New Alliance), in moral teaching (e.g. stress on conversion, purity, charity), in piety (e.g. sentiments of humility and confidence) and in matters of doctrine and belief (e.g. "Children of Light" and "Children of Darkness")? We hope to give some answers to these questions in the chapters which follow.

CHAPTER TWO

Resemblances between the New Testament and the Qumran writings should not surprise us. For one thing, it is only to be expected that there will be certain likenesses between two such organized religious bodies as the community of Qumran and the Church of the New Law, both of them "seeking" the true God and striving to be perfect, each in its own way. Both owed much to the Old Testament, and drew upon it as a common source. Need we repeat that the revelation of the New Testament was not, so to speak, built up on a vacuum? The Almighty did not make use of a new language, a language from heaven, to convey the mysteries of the Christian faith. Christ said truly, "I am not come to destroy the Law and the Prophets, but to fulfil" (Matt. 5:17)—the Old Testament basis was there, its language was used, though with a fullness of new meaning; its revelation was supplemented with new and deeper mysteries, its moral law perfected, the material types of its

30

legislation and cult were fulfilled in the Church of the New Law with its divinely-constituted hierarchy and sacramental system, deriving its efficacy from the one perfect oblation of the cross. Contemporary Judaism, too, sheds much light on the preaching of Christ and the apostolic writings; Strack and Billerbeck were able to fill four volumes with material illustrative of the New Testament from Jewish traditions later collected in the Talmud and Midrashim.[1] Even the apocryphal writings of the Old Testament, which were held in great favour by the sectaries, were not without their influence. It is well known that St. Jude in his epistle, written in the sixties of the first century, quotes the apocryphal Book of Henoch (vv. 14-15), and possibly, too, the Assumption of Moses (v. 9). Certain of these writings were well known among the early Christians, to such an extent that they freely interpolated them.[2] In fact, scholars have long ago indicated the points of contact that exist between the Apocrypha and the New Testament, or, for that matter, between Essenism and Christianity.[3]

POINTS OF CONTACT: ORGANIZATION AND PRACTICES

In comparing the scrolls and the New Testament, one might simply take the inspired writings in sequence and

31

indicate the more obvious parallels. Yet this method has its disadvantages, one of which is the danger of mistaking verbal resemblances for fundamental similarities and even dependence of ideas. A better approach, without altogether discarding the question of historical succession, is to proceed by way of subject-matter, examining the supposed similarities under such heads as organization, piety, moral teaching, doctrine and religious philosophy.[4]

In the first place, some interesting points of contact have been indicated between the organization and common practices of the Qumran sect and those of the early Christian communities, especially those of Jerusalem and Judea. "In the Christian Church, just as in the Essene Church," writes M. Dupont-Sommer, "the essential rite is the sacred meal, whose ministers are the priests. Here and there at the head of each community there is the overseer, the 'bishop.' And the ideal of both Churches is essentially that of unity, communion in love —even going so far as the sharing of common property."[5]

Most striking perhaps, and a practice for which no certain Old Testament parallel can be adduced, is that of community of possessions which obtained, for some time at all events, in the infant Church in Jerusalem. It was a practice linked with a spirit of brotherly love not unlike that of the sectaries: "now the multitude of believers were of one heart and one soul, and not one of them said that anything he possessed was his own, but they had all things in common . . . and all that believed were together and had all things in common. Their possessions and goods they sold and divided them to all, according as everyone had need" (Acts 4:32 and 2:44-5). The picture is completed by the trait of continuing steadfast in the apostles' teaching, and in the fellowship, in the breaking of bread and common prayer (Acts 2:42). There is no need to stress the similarities with the Qumran community as described in our previous article; the very word "yahad" (community), as Dupont-Sommer and others have pointed out, evokes the idea of the Christian *koinonia* (fellowship) of Acts, the Pauline Epistles and St. John's first Epistle.[6] Professor Coppens does not hesitate to suggest, apropos of the community of possessions, the hypothesis that certain of the sectaries were among the early Christian converts and introduced some of their practices into the new communities.[7]

This is certainly possible, but I do not think it likely. For one thing, as noted in my previous chapter, the sect continued in its strict isolation, and the jealous guardianship of its writings, beliefs and practices till the time of the Jewish Revolt of A.D. 66-70. Even if we grant, as

33

some do, the possibility of indirect influence by way of diffusion of ideas,[8] there are notable differences, both as regards practice and spirit, between the Jerusalem Church and the Qumran people over this question of community of property, as indeed, over some other practices which seem alike. In the Jerusalem Church it seems to have been a question of immovable goods, houses, land etc. (cf. Acts 4:34 and the cases of Barnabas and Ananias and Sapphira, 4:36 and 5:1 ff.). There was nothing compulsory about it, as St. Peter explained to Ananias (Acts 5:4). It seems to have been simply a transient phase of the first communities, which owed its origin to that initial fervour that strove to practise to the full the counsels of Our Lord regarding poverty and detachment. This does not, of course, exclude a practical objective, viz., to relieve poverty and want among the lower classes of converts. At Qumran, it was a question of all one's possessions and salary, something of strict obligation for all who undertook the oath of the New Alliance. The practical purpose of the common fund, according to the Damascus Document, was not to meet the general needs of the community so much as to have a kind of "social security" fund to provide for the old, the sick and the infirm, in a word, for all unable to work and thus chargeable to the community.[9] The source and spirit of the practice differed from that of

34

the Christian Church—it arose, not so much from the generous practice of a revealed counsel, as from the fundamental exclusiveness of the sect. The sectaries' possessions—even as their very persons and talents— must be effectively separated and withdrawn from the impure goods of those outside, so as to mark them off from the "sons of iniquity."

Similarly, as we shall realize more fully later, the "fellowship," the mutual love of the first Christians, differed in spirit from that of the sectaries, who undertook to "love all the sons of light," while yet "hating all the sons of darkness." For the origin of the common prayers and blessings of the early Jewish converts, whether in the Temple or in their own houses, we need not look beyond the ordinary practices of contemporary Judaism.

What of the sacred repast, which seems to have been the principal common religious practice of the Qumran community and which, among the Essenes, so Josephus tells us, took the place of the ritual banquet in the Temple? Had it any relation to the Christian "breaking of bread" (Acts 2:42) which, so we read in the Epistle to the Corinthians, frequently took the form of a common meal, a "love-feast" (*agape*), followed by the celebration of the Eucharist? Here again there is a Jewish basis for the holding of meals in common, in a spirit of fraternal charity, meals that were more or less sacred in character.[10] The practice is attested in the Jewish world at large, quite apart from Qumran and the Essenes. Yet there, of course, the resemblance ceases—there is no parity between the "table of the Lord" which "shows forth the death of the Lord till he come" (1 Cor. 10:21 and 11:26) and the common meals whether of the sectaries or of other Jewish groups.

There is no real parity, either, between Baptism, the rite of Christian initiation, preached and administered from the first Pentecost, and the ablutions and purifications of the Qumran sect. The "Rule" has much to say of the various "lustrations"—bathing, whether in river or cistern, washing, sprinkling—and attributes a certain purificatory value to them: the man who refuses to enter the Alliance "may not be purified by expiations or washed by lustral waters; may not be sanctified in the pools and in the rivers, not purified by any water which washes. He will remain unclean . . ."[11] Yet it is abundantly clear that there is no *ex opere operato* efficacy attached to these rites. None of them is of any use to the man who refuses to take the oath of the Alliance. He who does enter will be inwardly purified only gradually, through continued fidelity to the precepts of the Alliance, though complete purification, in body and spirit, will be realized only at the Day of Judgment, by direct act of God.[12]

What of the religious superiors of the Qumran community? The head of the community, in all probability a priest, is designated by titles—*Mebaqqer, Paqid*—which have the same fundamental meaning of "overseer," "superintendent" as the word *episkopos* used to designate the chief of the Christian churches. He is teacher and ruler, examines and admits new members, governs, judges, presides, sees to money matters. He must love his subjects "as a father loves his children" and must bear "all their sorrows as does a shepherd for his flock," lest "any be oppressed or overburdened in the congregation."[13]

Many of these resemblances might be expected in the nature of things in the case of religious communities. Moreover, surface resemblance often conceals fundamental differences. The Qumran leaders were teachers inculcating a "knowledge" and "wisdom" which turned around the revelation and events of the Old Testament, and the so-called "mysteries" of the sect, chiefly allegorical and often far-fetched interpretations of Scripture, peculiarities of calendar, community rites and practices.[14] The apostles were "witnesses" to the unique facts of the coming, life, teaching, death and especially

37

resurrection of Jesus, Messiah and Son of God. They were, as St. Paul tells us, "ministers of Christ and dispensers of the mysteries of God" (1 Cor. 4:1), teachers of the unique revelations of the Christian religion, dispensers of the Christian sacraments, Baptism, Confirmation, the Eucharist, for which there is no parallel at Qumran.

The Christian title *episkopos*, quite apart from classical usage which might have afforded a basis for the name, is found in the Septuagint Old Testament, rendering the Hebrew *Paqid* (overseer), applied to rulers, chief officers, magistrates, etc. The metaphor of "shepherd," applied both to the Qumran leaders and the Christian *episkopoi*, is also found already in the prophecies of Ezechiel and Deutero-Isaias.[15] Its usage among Christians surely derives especially from Christ's application of the metaphor to himself (John 10:1-30), and his subsequent delegation of his power over the whole flock to Simon Peter (John 21:15-17). Nor does the Qumran use of the metaphor "father" evoke the idea of spiritual paternity, through the preaching of Christ and the administration of the Christian sacraments, of which St. Paul speaks: "for in Christ Jesus by the Gospel have I begotten you" (1 Cor. 4:15; cf. Gal. 4:19 and Philemon 10).

Office among the Qumran community was not for life;

in fact the "overseer of all the camps" was compelled to retire at the age of fifty.[16] Other points of considerable difference could be noted; e.g., the Qumran overseer must have "an eternal hatred for the men of perdition"[17] —his role of shepherd, father and teacher is very much restricted to his own community.

NAMES AND TITLES

Another field in which points of contact arise between the Qumran scrolls and the New Testament is that of the names or titles used by the sectaries and by the first Christians. As indicated in the last chapter, the sectaries, living in the fifth and last age of the world, regarded themselves as the veritable "remnant" of Israel of which the prophets spoke, the only true Israel, "Aaron and Israel" simply, the "house of fidelity," the "house built by God," his veritable "Sanctuary" more than the material Temple of Jerusalem, God's chosen "plantation."[18] One of the earliest titles of the Christian Church was the "Israel of God" (Gal. 6:14). In the course of a passage in which many resemblances have been noted with the scrolls, St. Peter refers to his readers as a "chosen race, a royal priesthood, a holy nation . . . who

39

in times past were not a people, but are now the people of God" (1 Peter 2:9-10).[19] St. Paul refers to his converts under the metaphor of "planting"—a metaphor, incidentally, already used by Christ Himself (1 Cor. 3: 7-8 and Matt. 15:13); the metaphor of "house of God" is met with in St. Paul, in Hebrews and in Peter, and that of the "Temple holy in the Lord" also occurs in the Pauline epistles.[20] Striking though these similarities are, they can, and I think, should, be referred back simply to the Old Testament as a common source—who will maintain that St. Paul and his fellow-apostles were less well versed in their Scriptures than the monks of Qumran?

Somewhat the same should be said about the use of the title "The Elect," "Elect of God," in the Qumran documents.[21] "Elect of God" is also the name applied by St. Paul to the early Christians.[22] This title too derives from a common Old Testament source (cf. Isaias 65:23, etc.), and its meaning is not the same in the two cases. The Qumran sectaries are God's "elect" in a restricted and national sense, based on the election of the Chosen People at Sinai, issuing in the blessings of the Old Law, and on the conviction that they alone now represent and constitute that people. Christian "election" is, of course, a much broader and deeper thing, extending to embrace all believers, Jew and

40

Gentile, based on the new and eternal Covenant sealed with the blood of the Son of God, issuing in blessings of a far higher order than those of the Mosaic Law.

The sectaries of Qumran were wont to refer to themselves as the "holy assembly," God's "holy house," his "holy people," or simply "the Saints" or "Saints of the Most High."[23] Here is another interesting resemblance with the primitive Church of Jerusalem, the members of which were the first to be referred to by the distinctive title "The Saints,"[24] though the appellation was later used by St. Paul for the Churches of Asia Minor, Greece and Italy. Still, once again, we can find an Old Testament basis for the common use of this title. Several texts speak of Israel as a "holy people," as "holy men," and they are exhorted to be saints, to be holy even as their God is holy.[25] We may note in particular the prophecy of Daniel which characterizes the faithful remnant of the future as the "saints of the Most High" (Dan. 7:25 and 27), the very expression which the sectaries used. The People of the Old Law were "Saints" in so far as they were separated from all other nations in a unique alliance with the true God; they remained "Saints" inasmuch as they kept the Law which regulated the alliance. This is precisely what the Qumran community claimed to be and to do in a full and perfect manner. Needless to say, the "sanctity" of the first

Christians was not based on the election of Sinai, on the Mosaic Alliance and Law, but on a new vocation, a new economy of grace—for they were called to share in the fruits of Christ's redemption in his Mystical Body (cf. Rom. 8:28), as members of the Church, as walking "holy and unspotted in charity" (cf. Eph. 1:4).

Finally, we have the title "New Alliance," the equivalent of the *kaine diatheke* ("New Testament") of St. Luke, St. Paul and Hebrews.[26] In the Community Rule, to enter the Community is to "enter the Alliance" to become "men of the Alliance"; in the Damascus Document the expression "New Alliance (in the land of Damascus)" is used, also probably (the text is mutilated) in the Habacuc Commentary.[27] We know that St. Paul speaks of himself and his fellow-workers as "worthy ministers of the New Alliance"; the Epistle to the Hebrews devotes much space to this "New Alliance" established by the Sacrifice of Christ, and the same expression is met with in the account of the institution of the Eucharist at the Last Supper.[28]

In the first place, as ever, we can point to a common source for the expression in the prophecy of Jeremias (31, 32). More telling is the vast difference that underlies the verbal similarity. The Christian "New Alliance" was effectively established for all men through the blood of Christ, shed in sacrifice on Calvary, and there-

42

by the Old Alliance, concluded between one people and their God at Mount Sinai and sealed by the blood of animal victims, was abrogated. Now, the "New Alliance" of Qumran is nothing more than a renewal, however complete, of this old alliance of Sinai. As narrated in Deut. 29, 30, Moses had aready renewed the Alliance on the plains of Moab before his death; he foretold the future defection of the people, yet held out hope of further "renewals" of the Alliance. A very solemn renewal of the Alliance, we know, took place under Esdras and Nehemias after the Exile (Neh. 9, 10). Basically, the Qumran alliance is just another such renewal. The very ritual provided in the Rule for "entering the Alliance"—confession of sin, recitation of the blessings and curses attached to the Law, oath of loyalty[29]—is but the putting into effect of the prescriptions for renewal of the Alliance detailed in the closing chapters of Deuteronomy.

PIETY

In their Thanksgiving Hymns, and in the lyrical ending of the Rule, the Qumran hymnists manifest sentiments of religion and piety which do them honour. Of

43

the Thanksgiving Hymns, some, like many of the canonical Psalms, are prayers of the "poor man," giving thanks to God for deliverance from his enemies, foretelling and, be it said, rejoicing, in their divine chastisement. Others laud God as Supreme Creator and Master of human destiny. He alone is just and holy; before him man is but clay and his justification comes from God alone:

"As for me, I know that justice belongs not to man,
    Nor perfection of ways to the son of man.
To God Most High pertains every just work,
    Whilst the path of man is not made firm,
Save by the spirit which God hath created for him
    To make perfect the ways of the sons of men,
So that all creatures may know the might of his power
    And the greatness of his goodness to all the children of his
        mercy."[30]

It is in the lyrical ending of the Rule that the religious sentiment of Qumran attains its high water mark. We can but quote a few lines:

"I say to God, 'My Justice,'
    to the Most High, 'Author of my good, source of knowledge,
        fount of holiness, height of glory, omnipotence of eternal
        splendour!'"
"Justice belongs to God, and from his hand comes perfection
    of conduct,
    By his knowledge all things exist,
    By his plan he determines every being, and without him
        nothing will be made.

44

As for me, if I stumble, God's graces will come to my aid for
ever . . .
With his mercies he will reach me,
And according to his graces will he carry out my judgment . . .
In his justice will he purify me from all mortal sully,
That I may praise God for his justice, and the Most High for
his majesty."
"Blessed be thou, my God, who dost open the heart of thy
servant to knowledge . . .
Thou hast taught all knowledge; all that exists has come into
being through thy good pleasure,
Besides thee there is none other who can decree contrary to
thy Will,
Who can grasp all thy holy plans and the might of thy power.
Who can bear thy glory? What is the son of man among thy
marvellous works,
And the offspring of woman, how can he stand before thee? . . .
He is not rock, he is but kneaded clay and tends but to dust.
What shall the clay answer to the hand that fashioned it?
What (divine) thought could it comprehend?"[31]

No one will deny the loftiness and sincerity of these
sentiments, which sum up much of what was best in
Jewish piety and prepare the way for the Christian
revelation—"authentic religious attitude, the breath of
the Spirit which prepares in the wilderness the ways of
God," as Vermès puts it.[32] M. Dupont-Sommer goes
further: "If the spiritual songs of the New Alliance
retain the expressions of the Old Alliance, the general
sense and spirit are different. In actual fact, it is new
wine that has been poured into old bottles." And he

45

says further that they "are exactly comparable with the ancient Christian hymns which are to be found inserted in the Gospel according to St. Luke—the Magnificat, the Benedictus and the Nunc Dimittis."[33]

Beautiful though these Qumran Canticles are, I do not think that they depart from the broad general trend of Old Testament piety. Where, in fact, does one find among them those lofty outpourings on "communion with God" which are to be met with in certain of the canonical Psalms?—"The Lord is my shepherd, I shall not want . . . As the hart panteth after the fountains of living water, so doth my soul pant after thee, my God . . . I shall appear before thy sight in justice, I shall be satiated when thy glory doth appear . . . For what have I in heaven, and, apart from thee, what do I desire on earth? . . . Better is one day in thy courts above a thousand . . ."[34] The Qumran Psalms, like the other sectarian writings, are coloured, so to speak, by the rigid exclusiveness of the sect, their narrow view of predestination, their sharp and inexorable distinction between Sons of Light and Sons of Darkness. What can they show, then, to match the "broad sweep" of Psalm 116: "Praise the Lord, all ye nations: praise him, all ye peoples . . ."? What have they to compare with the magnificent Psalm of the "reign of Yahweh"—"Sing ye to the Lord a new canticle, sing ye to the Lord, all the earth . . . The Lord hath reigned, let the earth rejoice, let many islands be glad . . ." (Ps. 95:1; 96:1; cf. Ps. 94:97-9)?

It is well known that the canticles of Luke 1-2 are full of Old Testament allusions. For all that, there are many points in them which mark them off from the *Hodayoth* of Qumran, whose authors still grope, as it were, in the uncertain light of the Old Law. These New Testament canticles reiterate the joyful theme, "The Messiah is here!"—"The Orient from on high hath visited us . . . He hath regarded the lowliness of his handmaid . . . mine eyes have seen thy salvation . . . Blessed be the Lord God of Israel: because he hath visited and wrought the redemption of his people . . ." (Luke 1:78, 48, 68; 2:30). Here is true Messianic salvation: the enemy is not a human foe or persecutor, but sin—"to give knowledge of salvation to his people, unto the remission of their sins" (Luke 1:77). The light of Messianic salvation shines, not within the close limits of a seclusive sect, not even within the bounds of the Chosen Race, but over the whole world: ". . . thy salvation, which thou hast prepared before the face of all peoples, a light for the revelation of the Gentiles, and the glory of thy people Israel" (Luke 2:32); "all generations shall call me blessed . . his mercy is from generation to generation to them that fear him . . ." (Luke 1:48, 50 ff.).

Nor may the piety of the Qumran sect be compared

with that filial piety of Christians, of which St. Paul speaks; that piety, whereby, becoming God's children by divine adoption through the death of his Son, we cry, "Abba, Father!" (Gal. 4:6); that piety which finds its source in the abiding presence of the Holy Ghost in the hearts of the faithful—"For you have not received the spirit of bondage again in fear; but you have received the spirit of adoption of sons, whereby we cry Abba (Father). For the Spirit himself gives testimony to our spirit that we are the sons of God" (Rom. 8:15-16; cf. Gal. 4:4-5).

MORAL TEACHING

The realm of moral teaching is one in which we would naturally expect to meet similarities between Christianity and the Qumran sect, both of them, to a greater or less extent, using the Old Testament moral teaching as a foundation. Moreover, it is true to say of the sectaries that, in many respects, their "justice aboundeth more than that of the Scribes and Pharisees" (Matt. 5:20). It would be an interesting task—though beyond the scope of this book—to compare the moral life of the sectaries with the strictures applied by Christ to the Pharisees in the Sermon on the Mount and elsewhere, especially in the great "comminatory discourse" of Matthew 23. The comparison is very much in favour of the sectaries.[35]

To what extent, then, can we say of the Qumran people that they were "not far from the Kingdom of God" (Mark 12:34)? Much of the legislation in the Rule and the Damascus Document concerns matters of discipline and ritual, whilst elaborate penal codes list external faults and their penalties. Still, even in the legal passages, the moral virtues—obedience, purity and charity—are not neglected; whilst in the passages that concern the purpose of the Alliance, and especially the way of life that should characterize the "son of light," we have a full moral and ascetical teaching. Three "fundamental attitudes," declares Canon Coppens, link the moral outlook of the sect with that of the New Testament, viz., a radical opposition to impurity, a marked hostility to riches, and a generous effort to practise brotherly love and to conquer faults against charity.[36] Moreover, the "way of perfection," it is argued, follows the same general lines in the sect as with the early Christians: beginning with conversion and repentance, it continues in an uninterrupted warfare between the flesh and the spirit; it tends to the ideal expressed in the notions of justice, truth and charity, and issues in, finally, the distinction between the Sons of Light and the Sons of Darkness. All these points call for closer examination.

First, then, the radical opposition to impurity. The sectaries laid great stress on purity, and not simply ritual or legal purity but inward cleanliness, "circumcision of the heart," "pure lips," abhorrence of sexual impurity and immodesty and (in all probability) the actual practice of celibacy.[37] It is this latter point which goes beyond the demands and general trend of Old Testament morality and so is worth delaying over. It must be admitted that the motive and spirit underlying the practice of celibacy in Qumran differed from those of the New Testament. Christ counselled voluntary celibacy and virginity "for the Kingdom of God" (Matt. 20:12); St. Paul praised virginity that was entered upon for the love of Christ, that the generous Christian might be concerned "about the things of the Lord, how he may please God" (1 Cor. 6:32; cf. vv. 25-35). In the Qumran sect, the practice of celibacy—obligatory on all who took the oath—seems to have been motivated by legal considerations, viz., the avoidance of all ritual impurity, which was scarcely conceivable in the married state, and also by practical considerations, that is, the obvious difficulty of keeping the rigid rule of Qumran if the candidate brought his wife and family into the community with him! Finally, we must remember that the practice of voluntary celibacy for a religious motive was not without precedent in Israel; the cases of the prophets Elias, Eliseus and Jeremias are well known.

Secondly comes the "marked hostility to riches"; one feature of this—community and separation of property —has already been noted. In general it may be said that the Christian attitude to riches and possessions and the spirit of Christian detachment therefrom differed notably from the attitude of the sect. Christ did not condemn riches, though he emphasized how difficult it was for the rich man to enter the kingdom of God. He exhorted his followers to inner detachment from riches, and proposed as a counsel of perfection that they "leave all things and follow" him. It was for the sake of the kingdom of God, for the Messianic Kingdom which Christ came to establish, that Christians practised this detachment and in many cases freely renounced their possessions. The monks of Qumran looked on the stripping oneself of one's possessions as a *sine qua non* of salvation; possessions were renounced, not for the sake of the kingdom of God, but on account of the legal sully their possession entailed, till they were finally merged with the pure goods of the community. Community solidarity, complete separation of God's "elect" from the "sons of darkness"—such was the spirit animating this, and, indeed, so many other aspects of the moral theology of Qumran.

Brotherly love was held in high esteem, at Qumran. He who enters the Alliance must "love all the sons of light," love his neighbour as himself, seek his well-being, must not offend him by angry words, nor bring an accusation against him before he has been reprimanded before two witnesses.[38] They must "correct one another, as it is written," "reprimand one another in truth, in humility, and with benevolent love for each one"— passages which recall Christ's teaching on fraternal correction (Matt. 18:15-18).[39]

These sentiments are noble and not without some analogy to the mutual love of the early Christian *koinonia*, which compelled the pagans to exclaim: "Behold, how these Christians love one another!" Still, the charity of Qumran drew its inspiration, ultimately, from all that was best in the Old Testament, whereas Christian charity was based upon the sublime example and commands of the Son of God: "that you love one another, as I have loved you . . . that they all may be one, as thou, Father, in me, and I in thee . . ." (John 13:34-5 and 17, 21). Nor has the charity of Qumran the all-embracing sweep of its Christian counterpart. It is, in effect, limited to members of the sect. If the sectary is to "love all the sons of light," he is also bidden to "hate all the sons of darkness." The Rule has some hard things to say about those who refuse to enter the Alliance—they are worthy of contempt, outside the pale, as it were. The Damascus Document is still more severe with those "traitors" who abandon the Alliance, or oppose or refuse to listen to the teaching of the Teacher of Righteousness.[40] In fact, all communication with outsiders—save for necessary matters of buying and selling—is but sin and impurity. This is a far cry from the "love your enemies" and "teach ye all nations" of Christ, or from St. Paul's request for prayers for all men, seeing that there is but one God of all "who wills all men to be saved and to come to the knowledge of the truth."[41]

Now for the "way of perfection," beginning with conversion and repentance. The Qumran community consists of those who are "converted from their perverse conduct" and return with all their heart to the Law of Moses, confessing their sins in the rite of initiation. They are the "penitents of the desert" who went into the wilderness to "prepare the way of the Lord" and expiate in His sight the impiety of those outside.[42] There are obvious analogies with the New Testament, as, for instance, the preaching of John the Baptist, taken up again by Christ, "Do ye penance for the kingdom of God is at hand!" (Matt. 3:2 and 4:17). Nonetheless, the notions of conversion and repentance are a commonplace of the Old Testament—Law, Psalms and particularly the Prophets. The motive of repentance in the gospels is not that of a wholehearted return to the Law of Moses and the old alliance, but to enter the Messianic Kingdom of God—an idea scarcely mentioned in the Qumran documents.

It is, perhaps, not quite correct to speak of the way of perfection continuing in an "uninterrupted warfare between the flesh and the spirit" in the sect of Qumran. The opposition and enmity spoken of in the Rule is rather between the two "spirits," two ways of life, two opposed groups who follow their respective ways and spirits. True, we do read in the Habacuc Commentary that God will save the faithful of the New Alliance on account of "their sufferings and their faith in the Teacher of Righteousness," and elsewhere we read that the present time is a "season of affliction";[43] but this refers rather to external trials and persecution, than to that generous self-abnegation "for the kingdom of God" and "for Christ's sake" of which the gospel speaks. If the Rule speaks of the "penitents of the desert" expiating the impiety of wicked men, it is scarcely a question of vicarious satisfaction which obtains mercy and salvation for the sinner, for—according to Qumran theology— he is eternally doomed to perdition. The phrase seems to signify some kind of "off-set" in the eyes of God for the impiety of the "sons of iniquity," part and parcel of the perennial dualism between the spirit of light and that of darkness. We may note, finally, that the "flesh" is not "purified" till the end of time, by special act of God when he comes to judge.[44]

Then we have the "ideal expressed in the notions of justice, truth and humility." The concept of justice or righteousness is often met with in the Qumran scrolls. The sectaries are called "sons of justice," their master is the "Teacher of Righteousness (Justice)," and their vocation is "according to the plan of his (God's) justice." Their way is "to practise truth, justice, and right upon the earth."[45] With justice is coupled truth or fidelity, wholehearted allegiance to the Law of Moses and to their own doctrines, rules and practices. The sectaries are called "men of truth" and "sons of truth," their "hands must not weary in the service of truth even if the last times are prolonged," they must "keep fidelity on earth with firmness unshakeable."[46] In this they are opposed to the "sons of lying," just as their justice is opposed to the impiety of the "sons of wickedness." Humility, too, is linked with truth. The Rule exhorts to "truth, humble goodness, benevolent charity, right intention," to "a submissive spirit, longanimity, mercy, eternal goodness."[47] The sectaries apply to themselves

55

the expressions found in the Psalms to designate the humble man who trusts in God, viz., the "poor." They are "the simple of Juda who practise the Law."[48] As we have noted above, the Thanksgiving Songs and the lyrical ending of the Rule contain lofty sentiments on man's nothingness and powerlessness in the sight of God.

Not a great deal, however, need be said about similarities with the New Testament in these matters. The notions of justice, truth and humility in the senses explained are to be found in the Old Testament, especially the Psalms. The New Testament, St. Paul's epistles especially, uses the same expressions, but underlying them is all the difference we would expect between the New Testament and the Old. Justice with the sectaries is basically the perfect fulfilment of the Mosaic Law, not the carrying out of the more perfect teaching of Christ, as found in the Sermon on the Mount and elsewhere. Where the justice of God is spoken of, it is not the same as the justice of which St. Paul speaks in the Epistle to the Romans, a justice communicated to man through baptism and faith in Christ, inwardly purifying and adorning him with the grace of Christ. God's justice, according to the sectaries, is fully operative only at the end of time, when the righteous man is completely purified. Truth at Qumran is fidelity to the Law and the rules of the sect. Truth in the New Testament is founded upon that teaching so ably stressed by St. John and St.

Paul, the full revelation of the Son of God: "I am the Way, the Truth and the Life," the "Truth of the Gospel," "Truth of Christ,"[49] The Holy Ghost too, the "Spirit of truth," has clearly made known that truth to the Apostles.[50] The humility of the sect is a spirit of submissiveness to Community rule and authority, the patient acceptance of trial and persecution at the hands of wicked men. It is scarcely that absolute humility of the gospels and New Testament, the humility of little children before their Father, the sentiment of being the least of all "the offscouring of all"; it is not based on the teaching and example of the Son of God who said "The son of man is not come to be ministered to, but to minister and to give his life a ransom for many," and "learn of me for I am meek and humble of heart."[51] Nor was Qumran humility linked with universal charity, love even of enemies. This is not to say, of course, that the moral teaching of Qumran did not come near to Christ's teaching, indeed much nearer than that of the Scribes and Pharisees on these matters.

The question of "sons of light" and "sons of darkness" will be dealt with later. Enough for the present to say that the sanctity of Qumran was basically that of the Law, though enlivened with a "thirst for inward purity" which echoes some of the best passages in the Psalms and Prophets.[52] We do not meet that all-important factor in Christian sanctity—the presence of the

57

Spirit in the soul of the believer—"the love of God is poured forth in our hearts by the Holy Ghost who is given to us" (Rom. 5:5).

In our examination so far of the organization, piety and moral teaching of the Qumran sect, we have noted that, though the Qumran teaching frequently goes beyond that of contemporary Judaism, yet its roots are firmly fixed in the Old Testament, and, where verbal likenesses with New Testament notions are found, these should in nearly every case be referred back to the same Old Testament as to a common source. Underlying similar expressions, too, there is all that difference of meaning which we would expect between the Old Testament and the New. Even the most striking points of contact, e.g., those instanced between the sect and the infant Church of Jerusalem, do not, in my opinion, prove any real dependence or borrowing of ideas and terminology. The New Testament, which has a good deal to say about the Pharisees, Scribes, Sadducees, Herodians and other parties of Judaism, is silent regarding the Qumran community. Is it too much, then, to ask for solid proof before affirming any real contact between primitive Christianity and this sect? There remains, however, the very important matter of the doctrinal teaching of the sect. This we shall investigate in the next chapter.

CHAPTER THREE

In this chapter, we come to the question of the doctrines, the religious philosophy of the Qumran sect. In general it may be said that the sectaries were not greatly inclined towards religious speculation or well equipped for it. The "marvellous mysteries," "hidden things" and "revelations"[1] of which they speak turn out, upon examination, to be largely questions concerning the peculiar calendar of the sect, or distinctive interpretations of the Law and other sacred books, or relatively secondary matters such as the names of the angels. Original ideas are found in their teaching chiefly in the domain of angelology and eschatology, the doctrine of the "last things." In connection with the latter we have their distinctive doctrine on predestination, the two spirits and the two ways.

The question of angels, good and evil, is given some prominence in the Qumran writings, just as in the Old Testament apocrypha. Angels are classed into two main groups—good and evil—whose respective functions are very much linked with the fundamental teachings on the two spirits and the two ways. Thus, in the War Scroll, the names of the good angels are inscribed on the military banners of the "Sons of Light," and St. Michael is spoken of as their protector.[2] It may be that he, too, is the same as the great "Angel of Light," who guided Moses and Aaron, the "Prince of Light" in whose hands is the government of the "sons of justice."[3] The Almighty is surrounded by the "marvellous assembly" of his angels, and the sectaries look forward to praising him in their company at the end of time.[4]

On the other side, we find the evil angels under their chief, variously called Belial, Angel of Hostility, Angel or Prince of Darkness, in whose hands is the government of the "sons of iniquity."[5] The general impiety in Israel at the time of the founding of the Community is ascribed to the power of Belial;[6] in fact, he was looked upon in some sense as the cause of all sin, notably the past or present transgressions of the sectaries themselves. His power was directed especially to the destruction of the Community, against whom he constantly raised up persecution. Thus, in the "War Scroll," victory is thrice given by his power to the "sons of darkness," before God intervenes to give final victory to the "sons of light" in the seventh contest.[7] The enemies of the Congregation are the "congregation of Belial," who seek to ensnare it with the "plots of Belial," to engulf it in the "torrents of Belial," etc.[8] Yet, at the Last Day, the gates of Sheol will open to swallow up and imprison these spirits and all others who have "conceived iniquity."[9]

If in much of this there are points of contact with the New Testament—and we must remember that angelology is a relatively secondary doctrine in the New Testament —it must still be insisted that the doctrine of the sectaries is essentially based on the rather full Old Testament teaching.[10] Only in comparatively accidental points, e.g. the names and ranks of the angels, do we find a development, and this development is so much the common property of the various apocryphal writings, both apocalyptic and even rabbinical, that we may speak of it as part of the religious heritage of the Jewish world of New Testament times.[11] The question of the "two spirits" belongs more properly to the domain of eschatology.

It is well known that, in the latest books particularly of the Old Testament—such as Daniel, Machabees and Wisdom—we meet teaching on the Last Judgment, resurrection of the body, rewards and punishments after death, even on an intermediate state of purgation.[12] These ideas were taken up and developed somewhat by the apocrypha, and it has been claimed that the Qumran documents exhibit the furthest stage of this development.[13] Parallels with New Testament teaching have been cited under the following heads: belief in a catastrophe leading to the end of the world and the definitive salvation of the "elect"; the fate of the just and the wicked—the former join the society of angels to praise God in "eternal life," whereas the latter are punished in the "obscurity of eternal fire"; a participation by the "elect" in God's judgment.[14] Verbal parallels, too, have been cited, none, it must be admitted, entirely convincing, e.g. for the "light of life" (John 3:36), the "man of sin" and the "mystery of iniquity" (2 Thess. 2:3 and 7).[15]

In appraising these points of contact, we must bear in mind, first that the eschatology of Qumran is incomplete, even by Old Testament standards; e.g. there is no certain reference to the Resurrection of the Body. As regards the New Testament, to take simply the teaching of Christ in the Synoptic Gospels, there is no description of the Last Judgment to compare with Matt. 25, nor, indeed, anything on a par with the Discourse on the Last Things, the "Synoptic Apocalypse" of Mark 13 and parallels. The points of contact detailed above can all be found in the body of apocalyptic literature and would seem, just as in the case of angelology, to have been themes well known to the Jewish world of Our Lord's day.[16] Above all, the central theme of Christian eschatology, belief in the Parousia or Second Coming of Christ, finds no place in the teaching of Qumran. On the contrary, the sectaries held, apparently, that the first and only coming of the Messiah, which they believed to be near at hand, would herald the End of the World, when God himself would judge all men and admit his elect into eternal life. The Qumran monks looked forward to the full possession of Messianic blessings, complete purification and sanctification, only at the end of the world. Christians—through the redemptive death of Christ, the new covenant, the spiritual re-birth of Baptism, the coming of the Holy Spirit—already possessed by anticipation these heavenly Messianic blessings. St. John especially gives prominence to these ideas, sometimes referred to as "realized eschatology," viz. that the true

63

believer already has here below a life which is eternal, whereas "the world is already judged."[17] "It is," writes Canon Coppens, "both the mystery and paradox of Christianity to believe in this spiritual anticipation of the eschatological reign of God, being realized in the heart of the faithful and in the Church, in the course of a process wherein the practice of perfection, the reception of the sacraments, religious experience sometimes mystical, all play their part."[18]

Still, we do meet expressions in the Qumran writings which suggest a certain anticipation of eternal blessings. The Community is an "eternal planting," an "eternal assembly," with an "eternal inheritance"; its members pursue "eternal knowledge," "eternal peace," "eternal goodness."[19] These ideas have been compared to New Testament texts such as the following: "this is eternal life, to know thee, the only true God. . . ." (John 17:3); "in whom believing ye were sealed with the promised Holy Spirit, who is the pledge [first instalment] of our inheritance . . ." (Eph. 1:13, 14). Still, when we come to examine these expressions of the sectaries in their full context, we find that they do not signify any real anticipation of eternity, but simply a kind of destination to eternal life, a purposeful looking-forward to it. Thus, the Community is a "planting for eternity"; it is not yet an "eternal assembly," like that of the angels, but is destined one day to join them; the eternal heritage is still in the future. The knowledge they seek is a knowledge "for eternity"—they look forward to the perfecting of their knowledge and all their endowments at the Last Day. The goodness they strive after is also a "goodness which lasts eternally"—which includes, in fact, blessings which are both temporal (e. g. health, long life) and spiritual ("eternal life, a crown of glory with garments of splendour in the light for ever").[20] Likewise, as we shall see, the Spirit of God is poured forth in full measure only at the end of time. Thus eternal blessings are not enjoyed here below by the sectaries, save by way of figure of speech; whereas the Church of the New Testament actually begins with the effusion of the Holy Spirit, which the sectaries, so they believed, were to enjoy only at the End.

THE TWO SPIRITS AND THE TWO WAYS

What, meantime, of life here below? In an earlier chapter we sketched what we called the distinctive doctrine of the sect, viz., its teaching on the two spirits and the two ways, wherein walk respectively the "sons of light" and the "sons of darkness," each with their paths and eternal destiny rigidly determined by God from eternity. This conception, as we have tried to indicate, colours the piety, moral teaching and practices, organization, discipline, doctrine and religious philosophy of the sect. Before approaching the various parallels with the New Testament, it must be pointed out how alien is this whole conception to the teaching and spirit of Christianity, this "pessimistic conception which would paralyse the apostolate" as Canon Coppens puts it. The New Testament is filled with the spirit of confidence in God and in the power of his grace; he "wills all men to be saved"[21] and offers his grace through Jesus Christ to all men, Jew and Gentile. Hence the zeal of the apostles and their fellow-workers, their effort to preach the gospel to all men, in obedience to the command of Christ.

SONS OF LIGHT AND SONS OF DARKNESS

Yet it is precisely with regard to this teaching that most New Testament parallels, notably from the Joannine and later Pauline writings, have been cited. The theme of the contrast between light and darkness (in the moral sense) may be said, in fact, to run right through the New Testament. Our Lord himself, as recorded in the Synoptic Gospels, declared, "the children of this world are wiser in their generation than the children of the light" (Luke 16:8). In what is generally regarded as his earliest epistle, St. Paul, speaking of the "day of the Lord," exhorts his Thessalonian converts as follows: "But you, brethren, are not in darkness that that day should overtake you as a thief. For all you are children of light and children of the day. We are not of the night nor of darkness'" (1 Thess. 5:4-5). In Second Corinthians, he writes, "What fellowship hath light with darkness, or what harmony is there between Christ and Belial?" (6:14, 15). In Romans we read, "The night is passed and the day is at hand. Let us therefore cast off the works of darkness and put on the armour of light" (13:12). In the course of a famous passage on the Christian way of life in Ephesians (4:17-5:20), St. Paul writes: "You were heretofore darkness, but now light in the Lord. Walk then as children of the light. For the fruit of the light is in all goodness and justice and truth ... have no fellowship with the unfruitful works of darkness but rather reprove them ... but all things that are reproved are made manifest by the light: for all that is made manifest is light" (5:8, 9, 11, 13). Here, then, we have the "two ways," their respective spirits, works and fruits, and those that walk therein. "The contacts of vo-

67

cabulary of this passage with the 'Manual of Discipline' are numerous and manifest—one has the impression that the Apostle is addressing converts to Christianity from the Qumran sect"—this is the comment of Canon Coppens.[22]

St. Peter, too, writes of Christians, that they are "a chosen generation, a royal priesthood, a holy nation, a purchased people; that you may proclaim the perfections of him who has called you out of darkness into his marvellous light" (1 Pet. 2:9). However, it is especially in the Joannine writings that we seem to come nearest to the vocabulary of Qumran. In the fourth gospel the contrast of light and darkness is fundamental: "the light shineth in the darkness and the darkness could not comprehend [better, overcome] it . . . the Light hath come into the world, and men have loved darkness rather than light. . . . I am the Light of the world; he that followeth me walketh not in darkness."[23] By walking in the light, men become the "children of the light": "Yet a little while the light is among you; walk whilst you have the light . . . whilst you have the light, believe in the light that you may be the children of light."[24] Similarly, in the epistles of St. John, we read: "God is light and in him there is no darkness. If we say we have fellowship with him and walk in the darkness, we lie and do not the truth. But if we walk in the light, as he too is in the light,

68

we have fellowship one with another . . ." (1 John 1:6-7). As a practical instance, he states that he who loves his brother, walks in the light, whereas he that hates his brother is in darkness and walks in darkness (2:9-11). In the same epistle we have St. John's instruction on the "two spirits." The "test of the spirits" i.e. how, for practical purposes here and now, his listeners are to decide on the genuineness of those who claim charismatic gifts, is whether or not they confess that "Jesus Christ has come in the flesh." Yet the supreme test is "he that heareth God, heareth us: he who is not of God, doth not hear us: in this we know the spirit of truth and the spirit of error."[25]

If in all this, there are striking resemblances between the Qumran scrolls and the New Testament, yet the differences are no less striking. In the Qumran scrolls, it is an angel, the Prince of Light, that directs the children of light; in the New Testament, St. John especially, Christ himself is the Light and the Life. In the Qumran scrolls, the Prince of Light and the Angel of Darkness exist side by side without conflict; in St. John and St. Paul, Christ is attacked by the powers of darkness and triumphs over them, his triumph being consummated in his redemptive death and resurrection. For the sectaries, the "way of truth" is set forth simply as a moral and ascetical programme, which the "son of light" strives to

69

carry out by his own efforts; for the Christian, Christ has taken away sin by his death, and thereby introduces the believer into the kingdom and the paths of light, and by his grace assists him to walk therein. Briefly, the "two ways" of Qumran are embedded in the Old Law, those of the New Testament, in the New.

While admitting these considerations, Catholic scholars of note,[26] not to speak of many independent scholars, are so struck with the similarities of vocabulary instanced above that they admit that the New Testament writers, particularly John and Paul, borrowed formulae and expressions from the scrolls. Various theories have been evolved to explain the actual historical contacts between the Qumran monks and the early Christians.[27]

What are we to say? Let us take first the basic themes of light and darkness. In the Orient, where the brilliance of daylight is matched by the sudden onset of the darkness of the night, the metaphor of light and darkness is a fairly obvious one to choose. Thus, light is used in a figurative sense in the Old Testament in Isaias—a book much perused by the sectaries—to denote happiness and spiritual enlightenment (9:1), divine instruction and judgment for his people (10:17 and 51:4), and also the Messiah, Servant of Yahweh, in his office of teacher of the Gentiles (49:6; cp. 42:6). Here, then, ready to hand both for the monks of Qumran and the early Christians,

70

was a metaphorical usage of the idea of light to denote spiritual illumination as a result of divine instruction or revelation, be this the Law and Prophets or that of Christ. The concept of darkness, too, is used figuratively in Job to denote ruin (18:18), in Isaias to denote spiritual misery and ignorance (9:1 and 7:19). There is a particularly apt passage in the book of Proverbs about those "who leave the paths of uprightness to walk in the paths of darkness" (2:13).

Zachary was simply using the language of Old Testament Scripture, when, in his Benedictus, he said: "The Orient from on high hath visited us to enlighten them that sit in darkness and in the shadow of death" (Luke 1:78, 79). Christ himself, true Messiah of prophecy, takes up this thought and applies it to himself, investing it with a new and powerful meaning: "I am the Light of the world; he that followeth me walketh not in darkness" (John 8:12). Is it too much to seek the origin of St. John's—and also St. Paul's—insistence on the themes of light and darkness, in the beautiful and distinctive applications made by the Saviour himself?

True, the expressions "sons of light" and "sons of darkness" are not found in the Old Testament, but the material was ready to hand. "Son of such-and-such" is commonly used in the Hebrew scriptures to express a certain quality, attribute or tendency of a person; e.g.

"son of valour" is a valiant man, "son of death" a man worthy of death, "son of Belial" (i.e. perversity), a perverse fellow.[28] What more natural, then, than to call him who is illuminated spiritually, who follows the light, who is "begotten" by it, so to speak, a "son of light"— or him who rejects the light, whose mind and heart are darkened, who follows the counsels of the powers of darkness, a "son of darkness"?

Similarly, too, the immediate origin of the New Testament contrasts of truth and error, truth and iniquity, spirit of truth and spirit of error, may be sought in the words of him who said, "I am the Way, the Truth and the Life."[29]

THE HOLY SPIRIT

It was said in a previous chapter that the doctrine of the Trinity is not met with in the Qumran scrolls. Certainly, we find many references to the "Holy Spirit"— the sectaries are said to possess it, they must not profane it by unworthy conduct.[30] However, this is simply the human spirit or soul common to all men, albeit gradually purified in the Community by the elimination of evil inclinations and impure desires, by the practice of virtue, especially obedience to the Law and community rules, according to the programme of moral and ascetical life we have already sketched. This present "sanctification" prefigures and prepares for the eschatological purification.

Elsewhere there is mention of the "(Holy) Spirit of God."[31] This is to be communicated to the sectaries only at the end of time, to purify and sanctify them completely. The expression is not used in a personal sense, but in the sense in which it is commonly employed in the Old Testament, of an active attribute of God whereby he gives life, raises up and equips for their tasks judges, kings, prophets and psalmists, sanctifies and purifies.[32]

JESUS AND THE TEACHER OF RIGHTEOUSNESS

What of the Second Person of the Trinity? M. Dupont-Sommer, in his first work on the Dead Sea Scrolls, depicted the Teacher of Righteousness, who organized the Community, as a veritable prototype of Jesus, Messiah and Son of God. He argued that this Teacher, persecuted and martyred by the Wicked Priest, his adversary, was expected to rise again and return as Messiah and Judge. He was venerated as the "Anointed," the

"Unique One."[33] Not only, then, do we find in these scrolls, he wrote, a "whole theology of a suffering Messiah"—contrary to contemporary Jewish belief—but Jesus was himself "an extraordinary reincarnation of the Master of Justice."[34]

We do not deny that the Teacher of Righteousness was a priest, a master whose doctrines the sectaries must believe. But it is now pretty generally agreed upon that they did not identify him with the Messiah who was to come. There is no certain reference in the texts to the "Passion" of the Teacher of Righteousness,[35] still less to his resurrection or expected return. In the text "God by his elect will judge all nations" (*IQpHab* V, 4), "elect" should be read as elsewhere, as a plural[36]—the sectaries expect to assist at God's judicial act. In the text, "God, through his Anointed, hath made known his Holy Spirit" (*CDC* II, 12)—wherein M. Dupont-Sommer descried "something like a Trinitarian theology!"[37]—the reference, in the context, is not to the Messiah, but to Sadoq, eponymous ancestor of the sect. The Teacher of Righteousness is distinguished from the Messiah (or rather, two Messiahs, whom the sect awaited)[38] in the following text: "(traitors) will not be counted among the assembly of the people . . . from the day of the disappearance of the Teacher of the Community till the coming of the Messiahs of Aaron and Israel" (*CDC* XIX, 35-XX, 1).

74

The differences between Jesus and the Teacher of Righteousness are manifest. The Teacher neither claimed nor possessed the authority of Jesus as a teacher, nor was he conscious of powers placing him above the Law —he was simply its faithful exponent—and still less did he claim divine sonship. He worked no miracles. As a teacher he was not, as Jesus was, a master of parable, aphorism and logia, which might be faithfully remembered, collected and written down later by his disciples. What, too, of Jesus' predilection for the "publicans and sinners," that very category of men which the sectaries consigned to eternal perdition? Even in the persecutions to which Jesus and the Teacher were subjected, there are noteworthy differences. The enemies of the Teacher of Righteousness were anonymous, their identity veiled under the titles "Wicked Priest," "Prophet of Lying," etc. They were men of war and violence, impure, lovers of riches—in a word, violators of the Law. Jesus' enemies, on the other hand, are prominent and well-known —the Sadducees, Pharisees and Scribes. Far from being violators of the Law—and this applies especially to the last two categories, Christ's chief enemies—they were revered as its most assiduous exponents and upholders.

In passing, it may be noted that the sectaries had no great love for the "Davidic Messiah" of prophecy, whom Jesus claimed to be—they preferred to think of him (or them) as Messiah(s) of Aaron and Israel.[39] Nor is there anything but verbal similarity between "faith in the Teacher of Righteousness" (obedience to his laws and acceptance of his interpretations of Scripture) and that justifying "faith in Christ" of which St. Paul treats at length in Romans and elsewhere.

QUMRAN AND THE ESSENCE OF CHRISTIANITY

Truth to say, as we noted earlier, many of the most fundamental doctrines of the New Testament find no parallel in the Qumran scrolls; e.g. Redemption by vicarious expiation, the Blessed Trinity, the sacraments. Canon Coppens goes further and considers the "essence of Christianity" according to Christ's teaching, not indeed, as we understand it, but as it is understood by leading liberal scholars. As the essence of Christianity, some have reckoned God's tender love for the individual human soul, as preached by Jesus; others, a combination of Divine Fatherhood, universal fraternity and the coming and presence of the Kingdom; others, the presence of the Kingdom and hence the need for man to obey God's will absolutely.[40] Where, indeed, do we find parallels to these things in the Qumran writings? Is there anything to match the picture of God's universal tenderness as painted in the parables of the Good Samaritan and the Prodigal Son? Where do we find that spirit of "universalism" that pervades the New Testament, that sense of universal redemption issuing in the urge to preach the good tidings to all nations? The Kingdom of God, a fundamental notion in the synoptic gospels, is not even mentioned in the Qumran scrolls. There is only that vague idea of "domination," not of God, but of the angels who preside over the destiny of the "two ways."

CONCLUSION

To sum up the results of this tentative examination of the Qumran documents so far made known, our conclusions will fall under two headings: the light shed by the new documents on the background of New Testament times, and the problem of their possible influence on the sacred writers and early Christianity generally.

With regard to the first point, no one will deny the valuable and unexpected light which the new scrolls have shed on the Jewish world of the first century. They give us a first-hand picture of a kind of *tertium genus* in Jewish religious life, distinct from the parties of

Pharisee and Sadducee, an element previously known from sketchy allusions in various sources, but which had not till now yielded up its own writings. I refer—to use a general term—to the world of the Essenian movement. Here we meet much of what was best in Judaism: high ideals of moral life and piety, surpassing those of Scribe and Pharisee; a sincere quest for perfection within the bounds of the old dispensation, as instanced, e.g., in the practice of celibacy; an intense longing for the Messiah, not only as king but also as priest; a keen sense of the reality of the future life, with its eternal rewards and punishments. These things are not without importance in evaluating the Jewish background of the gospels, e.g. let no one now object against the virginity of Mary or her virginal marriage with St. Joseph that voluntary celibacy for a higher motive was a thing unheard of and morally impossible among the Jews of that time. Here and there, too, the text of the scrolls may serve to illustrate some Jewish practice mentioned in the gospels, e.g. dedicating one's goods to the Temple (*Qorban,* cp. Mark 7:11), or drawing one's sheep out of the pit on the Sabbath day (Matt. 12:11).[41] Here and there, too, additional light may be shed on the interpretation of certain texts, e.g. "peace on earth among men of good will" (Luke 2:14).[42]

The second point is more problematical. It is highly

improbable, to say the least, that Jesus and the Apostles, or even John the Baptist,[43] had any direct contact with the Qumran monks. Direct, causal influence of the Qumran writings on the origins of Christianity has been ruled out in the course of our investigations. Indirect influence —especially for the later New Testament writings—by way of a certain diffusion of ideas, as part of the general body of apocalyptic writings and notions, is possible, but not to be exaggerated. At most it concerns the vocabulary, the "periphery" of the New Testament. We cannot do better in conclusion than to quote the measured verdict of Canon Coppens, who, as we have seen more than once, is prepared to go some distance in admitting possible contact between the scrolls and the early Christian world: "Over against a Jewish sect, which did not succeed in disentangling itself from the bonds of ritualism, which was deprived of revelation flowing from a divine source and nourished itself instead upon a fantastic exegesis of texts from the Law and Prophets, there arises a new and dynamic religion in which the presence and the experience of the Spirit show forth a vitality that is unique. Even when this religion borrows expressions and formulae from its surroundings, a thoroughly new sense pervades the old terminology. By way of metaphor —if the first Christians did borrow from the sectaries a few 'organ-pipes,' the breath that now blows through them is that of the life-giving Spirit, the Holy Spirit, the Spirit of Jesus, he who searches all things, even the depths and mysteries of God, 'mysteries' very different from those secrets of calendar and chronology upon which the attention and speculation of the sectaries was largely concentrated."[44]

CHAPTER FOUR

A RECENT WORK ON THE SCROLLS

The most recent addition to the already formidable literature on the Dead Sea Scrolls is a work in English by the American literary critic, Edmund Wilson.[1] Though not himself a Biblical scholar, the author has been at pains to acquire full information; he has visited Qumran, interviewed the archaeologists and principal scholars concerned and read widely. He writes well and gives a fascinating account of the discovery and subsequent fate of the scrolls, and of the controversies that have arisen with regard to the sect that produced them (whom he identifies with the Essenes), its place in Jewish history and the question of its relationship with Christianity.

It is in connection with this latter point that the author

puts forward, somewhat tentatively yet with considerable literary skill, his own views, which resemble in many respects those first advanced by M. Dupont-Sommer, for whom he professes a certain admiration.[2] He indicates a number of parallels between the Qumran sect and the New Testament: resemblances in the teaching and expressions of the gospels, especially that of St. John;[3] the practice of Baptism, closely linked with doctrine on the Holy Spirit; the "Sacred Repast"; the doctrine of the Two Ways and of universal judgment by the Messiah, "doctrines unknown to the ancient Hebrews"; the doctrine of vicarious redemption or ransom, a teaching "cherished in the sect," for the Teacher of Righteousness "was persecuted, he does seem to have been regarded as a Messiah."[4] Hence he does not hesitate to affirm, "we know also that the rites and precepts of the Gospels and Epistles both are to be found on every other page of the literature of the Sect."[5]

JESUS AND QUMRAN

What, then, he asks, "was the relation of Jesus to the ritual and doctrine of the Sect, which the Gospels so persistently echo?"[6] He first notes, with apparent approval, the opinion of Brownlee and others that John the Baptist was adopted in the wilderness by the Essenes and moulded by them in accordance with their own principles.[7] Now Jesus also was born at Bethlehem, not far from Qumran, and was related to the Baptist on his mother's side. "Could he have been actually a member of the sect during those early years of his life when we know nothing about him?"[8] If the Teacher of Righteousness died a martyr's death and was regarded by the sect as one who fulfilled the Servant Prophecies of Isaias, "Jesus may well have found prepared for him, by the teaching of the Dead Sea sect, a special Messianic role, the pattern of a martyr's career, which he accepted, to which he aspired."[9]

Still, how are we to explain the striking contrast between the spirit of forgiveness and charity of the Gospels, and the "hate thy enemy," "hate the sons of darkness" of the Qumran writings? Wilson thinks that the Gospels and New Testament represent a kind of final stage in the lineal development of the religion of the sectaries. The first stage, represented by the Qumran documents generally, and the War Scroll in particular, is tinged with the "hate thy enemy" theme, or rather, the idea of political hostility, for the "sons of darkness" were probably the Romans.[10] The next stage is reflected to some extent in the Essenes of Josephus, who did not make weapons of war, and to a greater extent in the apocryphal "Testaments of the Twelve Patriarchs" in which "meekness and mercy are emphasized almost to the same degree that they are in the Gospels themselves."[11] Wilson suggests that the return of the sect to Qumran in 4 B.C., following the abandonment of the monastery due to the earthquake, marked the beginning of this new stage "in which the resentment of defeat is already giving way to resignation, the resignation of political helplessness," and where he who believes himself, or is believed to be, the Messiah "can preach only a moral salvation through faith in a non-militant God, and the righteousness of the individual."[12] The defiance of the Teacher of Righteousness, the pacifism of Josephus' Essenes, and Jesus' turning the other cheek would then mark successive stages in the adjustment of the Jews to defeat.[13] The Gospels are the final product, though "marked with occasional flashes of pugnacity"![14] "We can guess how, about half a century before its refuge was burned together with the Temple of the Jewish God, this movement had inspired a leader who was to transcend both Judaism and Essenism, and whose followers would found a Church that was to outlive the Roman Empire and ultimately be identified with Rome itself."[15] "This monastery, this structure of stone that endures, between the bitter waters and precipitous cliffs,

84

with its oven and its inkwells, its mill and its cesspool, its constellation of sacred fonts and the unadorned graves of its dead, is perhaps, more than Bethlehem or Nazareth, the cradle of Christianity."[16] "It would seem," he concludes on a later page, "an immense advantage for cultural and social intercourse—that is, for civilization—that the rise of Christianity should, at last, be generally understood as simply an episode of human history rather than propagated as dogma and divine revelation."[17] In proposing these theories the author wonders whether "the scholars who have been working on the scrolls—so many of whom have taken Christian orders or been trained in the rabbinical tradition—may not have been somewhat inhibited in dealing with such questions by their various religious commitments."[18] The inquirer without any religious affiliations "comes finally to ask himself whether anyone but a secular scholar is really quite free to grapple with the problems of the Dead Sea discoveries."[19]

CRITIQUE

At the risk, then, of "speaking as one less wise," as one whose "religious commitments" are very clear and definite, the present writer can but offer the following criticism, basing himself, as he has tried to do in previous chapters, on what seem to be the objective facts, on the one hand, of the Qumran scrolls, and on the other, of the New Testament.

First, then, a word about Wilson's method. Its great defect, to my mind, is its failure to give the ordinary reader a coherent picture of the Qumran sect *as a whole* —its organization, discipline, moral and religious teaching, as contained, for example, in the basic document of the Community Rule ("Manual of Discipline"). Quotations from the Qumran literature are few, and references to texts and authorities cited fewer still. The casual reader is left with the impression that the resemblances between the Scrolls and the New Testament are far greater than they actually are. Wilson's claim that the characteristic doctrines, rites and precepts of the gospels and epistles are reflected on every other page of the literature of the sect is not justified by the examples he gives, or by the facts of the case, as we have tried to show in this book. At the risk of repetition, we must recall that the writings of Qumran are firmly embedded in the framework of the Law of Moses, the old dispensation, the covenant of Sinai; the New Testament reposes on a new and universal covenant, mediated by the Son of God, a new order of things, alive with the breath of

86

the Spirit of God, of which the old was but a shadow. We have tried to show that the ablutions of the sect are not the same thing as Christian Baptism, nor is the "Spirit of God" the same as the Holy Spirit of the New Testament. The "sacred repast" of the sectaries has nothing which corresponds to the essence of the Christian sacrament and sacrifice. The Teacher of Righteousness was not regarded as the Messiah, nor is there anything in the texts to prove that the sectaries—any more than their fellow-Jews—believed in a "suffering Messiah" or in the doctrine of his redemptive death. In noting that the doctrine of the Two Ways is common to the Qumran writings and the New Testament, Wilson fails to draw attention to the totally different spirit that underlies the common terminology: in the New Testament, all men are redeemed, all called to be saved, to all the gospel is preached; in the Scrolls, in virtue of rigid and eternal determination, only the handful of elect Jews who enter the "alliance" are called to salvation, while the rest are doomed to perdition and denied the light of real truth and the means of salvation.

There is no real proof for that "development" of sectarian outlook of which Wilson speaks—the scrolls themselves, bearing abundant evidence of constant usage till the day they were hidden away at the approach of the Romans, contain no evidence of it, and surely they afford us an authentic picture of the sect from within, a picture that is more exact than the somewhat idealized accounts of the Essenes given by Philo and Josephus. Indeed, the fact that Josephus' Essenes did not make weapons is a somewhat slender basis on which to begin to erect a theory of religious evolution; for that matter, no weapons were found in the ruins of the Qumran monastery, save the arrow-heads of the Roman legions who destroyed the building in the first Jewish revolt. The equation "Children of Darkness" = "Romans" can scarcely be maintained from a reading of the Rule. Not only does it say that the two spirits dispute the hearts of all men, but the Jews themselves who refuse to enter the Alliance, and the traitors who turn back to walk again in "obstinacy of heart," are also reckoned among the "sons of darkness."[20]

As for the "Testaments of the Twelve Patriarchs," it has long been maintained that they have suffered from serious Christian interpolation. In fact it is now solidly held, on the basis of detailed examination of their whole structure, and careful comparison of the Greek, Syriac and Aramaic witnesses to the text, that they were actually a Christian work.[21] This conclusion seems to be confirmed by the findings in the Qumran caves—fragments of many apocryphal works have been found there (Henoch, Jubilees, Lamech in all probability, and others whose existence was unsuspected), but there is no trace of the Testaments as we now have it. "Given the extreme variety and richness of these (sc. Mss. finds), the pre-Christian and Palestinian origin of this apocrypha (i.e. the Testaments) seems thereby practically excluded." So writes Abbé Milik, one of the distinguished team of scholars working on the cave material in Jerusalem.[22]

WAS JESUS AN ESSENE?

Comparison of Christ's teaching and the documents of Qumran makes it clear that he did not derive his gospel from the Essenes. However, for the sake of argument, let us consider the suggestion that Jesus was trained at least for some time by these Jewish monks. Here, if nowhere else, it is imperative to take a thoroughly realistic approach to the whole question.

The Qumran sect, as explained in a previous chapter, was not a kind of seminary for the training of missionaries, but a rigidly enclosed monastery, a conventicle of the "elect," where a man worked out his own salvation by life-long effort. After being examined, he was required to take solemn oaths and then introduced by solemn rites to his "postulancy"; there followed a two-years' novitiate before he might, if suitable, be admitted to full membership and a share in all the common practices, being now effectively separated in person and property from the "sons of perdition." There he stayed, if faithful, for life, till finally he was buried in that simple cemetery overlooking the grim waters of the Dead Sea. There was to be no contact with outsiders for him, whether by way of "goods or counsel,"[23] he might not divulge the writings, rule, teachings, rites or customs of the sect to outsiders, his was to be "an eternal hatred for the men of perdition."[24] If then, Jesus—and the same would apply to the Baptist—had been a member of the sect, the only conclusion one can draw is that, breaking the solemn oath of admission, he had left it, or been dismissed—in either case falling under the formidable excommunication of the sect. He would be one of those who (in spite of monition, and period of penance, maybe) had "gone backward" and "walked again in obstinacy of heart," one of the traitors who had abandoned the paths of light to walk in the paths of darkness, excluded for ever from the elect "assembly of the people."[25] Anyone who had contact with him would fall under the same excommunication and irrevocable dismissal.[26] Is it too much to say, then, that this was scarcely the atmosphere in which we should expect to find that amicable rapprochement between the doctrine of the sectaries and the teaching of Jesus, which Wilson seems to postulate? Speaking humanly, one would expect, on the contrary, a good deal of disillusionment and a tendency in the opposite direction.

We can approach the matter from another angle, viz., what we know of the actual life of Jesus. True, we have few details on the early life of Jesus, but we do know that, after the return from Egypt, he lived at Nazareth with Mary and Joseph, and there we find him at the age of twelve years subject to them.[27] When his public life opened with his solemn manifestation at his Baptism and his subsequent victory over Satan in the wilderness, we are told "It came to pass in those days that Jesus came from Nazareth in Galilee and was baptized by John in the Jordan."[28] There followed the brief ministry in Judea of which St. John tells us in the first chapters of his gospel, then the return to Galilee and the preaching of the Kingdom of God after John the Baptist was cast in prison. The background of Jesus' early years seems to have been pretty well known to his Jewish contemporaries. His fellow-citizens of Nazareth, when he came to preach in their synagogue, were astonished at his doctrine and exclaimed, "Where did he get all this? What is this wisdom that is given him? Is not this the carpenter, the son of Mary, the brother of James and Joseph and Jude and Simon . . . ?"[29] When Jesus preached on the Bread of Life in the synagogue of nearby Capharnaum and claimed to be the Living Bread come down from heaven, the Jews objected, "Is not this Jesus the son of Joseph, whose father and mother we know?"[30] In reply, Jesus does not claim any affinity for his doctrine with that of any Jewish sect, Essene or otherwise, but appeals to a direct mission from the Father—no one comes to him, he says, unless the Father draws him, and he that listens to the Father, comes to his Son.[31] When he preached and made astounding claims before the learned Jews in the Temple of Jerusalem, they "marvelled, saying, how does this man come by his learning, since he has not studied?"[32] In reply, Jesus states that his doctrine is not "mine, but his who sent me."[33] Again and again in John's gospel there recurs this appeal to a direct mission from the Father as the source of his unique teaching and power.[34]

Even if—*quod absit*—Jesus was deceiving his contemporaries in this matter, one must take into account the machinations of his enemies. Surely, if he had been connected with the sect of Qumran—this exclusive, indeed schismatical sect, with its own calendar, rites, discipline and teaching, its claim to be the only true Israel— his enemies would not have failed to bring the matter up against him in public. Certainly, they neglected no means of trying to discredit him in the eyes of the people: they accused him of breaking the Law of Moses under several heads, they scoffed at his Galilean origin, they sought to entangle him in interpretations of the Law, they did not scruple at involving him in trouble with the Roman authorities, accusing him of forbidding the payment of tribute, of stirring up the people and claiming to be the Messianic king. To say the least, their silence on this question, like the silence of Jesus' friends and kinsfolk, demands some explanation, if he really had been once an Essene.[35]

WAS THE BAPTIST AN ESSENE?

Others, besides Wilson, have stated, with a good deal of assurance, that John the Baptist had been a member of the Qumran sect, and was thus in a position to acquaint Jesus with the teaching of the sect.[36]

Here again, the same practical difficulties that we detailed for the case of Jesus apply with the same force to the Baptist. Moreover, the facts of his parentage seem to render improbable the hypothesis that he would be attracted to the Qumran sect. His father, Zachary, was an orthodox priest, who ministered in the Temple of Jerusalem, his mother, Elizabeth, was likewise of the family of Aaron. Would he have been attracted to an exclusive and heterodox sect that valued its own rites higher than the Temple sacrifices, that had its own calendar, its own religious practices, its books, its initiations and excommunications? John's own relations later on to the authorities of Jerusalem were quite normal—he gave a reasonable answer to their deputation which inquired as to his credentials.[37]

In the picture painted by the gospels of John's birth and early years, we see him as a solitary, a divinely-called prophet, after the pattern of Elias of old. The Angel announced to Zachary that his son would go before the Lord "in the spirit and power of Elias" to prepare his people; to that end he was the object of God's predilection from his very conception—"he shall be filled with the Holy Spirit even from his mother's womb."[38] In his Benedictus Zachary prophesied of his child that he would be a "prophet of the Most High" to go before the face of the Lord and prepare his ways.[39] Soon after, we read that John was in the deserts till the days of his public manifestation[40]—again the picture of the solitary ascetic, preparing under the guiding hand of the Spirit of God for the great mission that would one day be his.

It was as the new Elias, with his clothing of camel's

hair, his leathern girdle and food of locusts and wild honey, that John began his public preaching. This preaching had a universal stamp about it that is wanting in the teaching of Qumran—all are called to Messianic salvation, even the publicans and soldiery, and the Pharisees are rebuked for arrogating to themselves the privileged position of being true "sons of Abraham."[41] John's preaching of repentance is based on a theme that has no parallel in the scrolls, viz., the Kingdom of God.[42] His baptism—which, more than all else, is cited as a borrowing from the sectaries—differs considerably from the ablutions of Qumran. It was a symbolic rite, clearly distinguished from the effective purificatory action of the coming Messiah;[43] it was a public testimony of repentance, "Baptism of repentance for the forgiveness of sins,"[44] a protestation of conversion on the part of the sinner who underwent it. Now, as was explained in an earlier chapter, the purificatory rites of the sect were not at all concerned with initial conversion and reception into the sect, when sins were publicly confessed and the solemn oaths taken. They were a kind of privilege reserved for the "Great," those who were fully initiated or at least were on their second year of novitiate. It seems clear that these rites were not an outward sign of repentance, nor, in fact, concerned directly with the remission of sin; they were part of the sectaries' quest for complete ritual purity, symbol of their utter segregation from men of impurity and their standing as the predestined elect of God. These differences are equally, if not more, valid in comparing the Qumran rites with Christian Baptism.

Moreover, John's baptizing seems to have been accepted by the Jewish world at large as a practice which occasioned no surprise. When the Temple authorities questioned him concerning his authority, it was not so much the baptism itself they queried, as his authority for so acting. "Why, then, dost thou baptize, if thou be not Christ, nor Elias, nor the prophet?"[45] When Jesus' disciples baptized later on, the complaint of the Pharisees was simply that Jesus was making more disciples and baptizing more than John.[46] Again, when Jesus, to outwit the machinations of the Temple authorities, put his own question to them, he was able to take the baptism of John as an accepted thing; he simply asked them about John's authority for so acting: "The baptism of John, whence was it, from God, or from men?"[47]

CONCLUSION

The candid reader who examines carefully the writings of Qumran and then turns to read the New Testament, cannot fail to be impressed with the tremendous gulf that separates the two sets of writing. In fact—and this is the opinion of the present writer, with all due deference to those sincere scholars who hold the contrary—the more one thinks over the matter, the more one grows sceptical over the whole question of direct contacts between the Qumran literature and the New Testament. And this is not, as Wilson remarks, following Brownlee, for fear "that the uniqueness of Christ is at stake."[48] Quite the contrary! The perusal of the scrolls side by side with the gospels and New Testament does but bring into greater relief the uniqueness of Christ and the transcendence of the religion which he founded.

Notes

NOTES ON CHAPTER ONE

1. The expression is used in a broad sense to designate all the manuscript material discovered in the Desert of Judea in the last few years, viz., at or near *Qumran* (1947, 1949, 1952) to the north-west of the Dead Sea; in the *Wadi Murabba'at*, further to the south, in 1951-52 (material mostly dated to the 2nd century A.D.); in the *Wadi-en-Nar* (ancient Kedron) in 1952 (chiefly Christian MSS.) and in another locality not determined with certainty in the same year (various material from the 1st century A.D. onwards). We use the expression here in a stricter sense, to designate the *Qumran* material.

2. *The Dead Sea Scrolls: a preliminary survey*, p. 98 (English translation 1952, of *Aperçus préliminaires sur les manuscrits de la Mer Morte*, 1950; New York, Macmillan).

3. Cited by H. H. Rowley, *The Listener*, 2 Dec. 1954. p. 957.

4. Ibid.

5. A. Dupont-Sommer, in his more recent work, *Nouveaux aperçus sur les manuscrits de la Mer Morte* (1953), p. 197.

Cited, and, to some extent, endorsed by F. M. Braun, O. P., in "L'arrière-fond Judaique du quatrième évangile et la Communauté de l'Alliance," p. 41, n. 1 (*Revue Biblique* 62 (1955)).

6. G. Kuhn: "Die in Palästina gefundenen hebräischen Texte und das Neue Testament," *Zeitschr. Theol. Kirche* 1950, pp. 192-211. W. Grossouw: "The Dead Sea Scrolls and the New Testament," *Studia Catholica,* 26 (1951), pp. 289-99; 27 (1952), pp. 1-8.

7. The best survey in English, complete up to mid-1952, is H. H. Rowley, *The Zadokite Fragments and the Dead Sea Scrolls* (Blackwell, 1952). A more recent work by a Catholic scholar, to which we are much indebted, is *Les manuscrits du Désert de Juda,* by G. Vermès (2nd ed., 1954).

8. The incomplete scroll of Isaias, the War Scroll and the Thanksgiving Songs were acquired by the Hebrew University, Jerusalem; extracts from them were published by Professor Sukenik in *Megilloth Genuzoth* (Vol. I, 1948; vol. II, 1950), and the complete texts were edited posthumously in *'Otsar hammegilloth haggenuzoth* (Jerusalem 1954). According to the latest system of abbreviations now adopted, these three scrolls are referred to as *IQIsb, IQM* and *IQH* respectively, *IQ* designating the first cave of Qumran, the other letters, the Hebrew name of the work, viz. Isaiah (2nd scroll), *Milhamah* (i.e., War) and *Hodayoth* (i.e., thanksgiving hymns.)

The remaining scrolls were acquired by the Syrian Metropolitan of Jerusalem, but were loaned to the Americans for safe-keeping and publication. They were published in *The Dead Sea Scrolls of St. Mark's Monastery* (2 vols., New Haven, 1950-1951). They are designated by the abbreviations *IQpHab* (i.e., *pesher* or explanation, of Habacuc), *IQS* (i.e., *Serek hayyahad,* rule of the Community) and *IQIsa* (first and complete scroll of Isaiah). A news report from Tel Aviv in March

1955 stated that these scrolls, together with the still-unopened scroll of Lamech (*IQLam*), have now been purchased by the government of Israel.

9. *Discoveries in the Judean Desert,* vol. I (Oxford University Press, 1955). This is the first of a projected series of seven or eight volumes which will make available all the fragmentary manuscript material that has passed through the hands of the Palestine Museum (Jordan).

10. However, there is now a fair measure of agreement among palaeographists for a broad dating between the 2nd century B.C. and the 1st A.D. Archaeologists in Jerusalem divide the scrolls palaeographically into two groups: the earlier group, comprising *IQIsa* and *IQS,* dates from the 1st century B.C.; the later, including the other four published scrolls, from the 1st century A.D. The *Murabba'at* documents, dated to the first part of the 2nd century A.D., have been of considerable help in establishing this palaeographical sequence.

11. Preliminary reports in *Rev. Bibl.* 60 (1953), pp. 83-106 (1951 season) ; ibid. 61 (1954), pp. 206-36 (1953 season) and pp. 567-8 (brief account of 1954 season). A short account of the completion of the work in 1955 was given by G. L. Harding in the *Illustrated London News,* Sept. 3, 1955, pp. 379-81.

12. Subsequent MSS. discoveries at *Murabba'at* and elsewhere, involving 2nd century material exhibiting a development both in script and in the Hebrew text of the Old Testament, served to confirm this conclusion.

13. See *Rev. Bibl.* 60 (1953), pp. 540-61.

14. Evidence for this in the shape of wooden tent-supports was found in one of the caves.

15. In cave 3Q were found two copper scrolls, which have not yet been unrolled, because of their very brittle condition. The imprint of Hebrew letters showing through on the outside

suggests that they had formed a plaque set up on the walls of some community room in Khirbet Qumran, a notice of some kind—or alternatively, as Professor Kuhn thinks, they contained an inventory of the Community property and possessions (see *Rev. Bibl.* 61 (1954), pp. 193-205). The delicate work of unrolling them has been entrusted to the College of Technology of the University of Manchester.

16. Origen tells of the discovery of Hebrew and Greek MSS., hidden in a jar, in the neighbourhood of Jericho, in 217 A.D.; there is record of another discovery of Hebrew manuscripts in a cave near the same city about the year 800; a later Jewish writer, Qirqisani, speaks of a Jewish sect known as "the men of the cavern," because their writings were found in a cave.

17. Known by the abbreviation *CDC* (Code of Cairo Damascus Covenanters), and first published by Schechter in 1910. It is significant that the synagogue in Cairo belonged to the Jewish sect of Karaites, a peculiar medieval sect that had many points in common with the Qumran sect. It has been plausibly suggested by many eminent scholars that a considerable part of the Qumran library, ransacked in antiquity, found its way into the hands of this sect.

18. Some, notably M. Dupont-Sommer, basing themselves on an obscure text of the Habacuc Commentary (XI, 4-8), think that the Teacher of Righteousness was put to death by his adversary. This interpretation is not generally maintained now.

19. *The Zadokite Fragments . . .*, p. 21. ..

20. Cf. Vermès, op. cit., p. 66.

21. Cf. art. "Esséniens" (*Dict. Bibl. Suppl.*, II, 1109-1132) and Vermès, op. cit., pp. 57-66.

22. *Hist. Nat.*, V., 17.

23. *Rev. Bibl.* 60 (1953), p. 105.

24. Identifications have been sought in Machabean and

Hasmonean times, in early Christian times and even in the Middle Ages. On these theories, see Rowley, op. cit., pp. 31-61 and Vermès, op. cit., pp. 67-9.

25. Cf. D. Barthélemy in *Rev. Bibl.* 60 (1953), p. 423 and R. De Vaux, ibid., 61 1954), pp. 630-1. It must be mentioned that Professor Rowley relates the activity of the Teacher of Righteousness to the period immediately preceding the Machabean revolt (the events of 2 Mach. 3-6) ; cf, op. cit., pp. 62-88. Precisely the same conclusions were reached independently by a Catholic writer, A. Michel, in his very full study, *Le Maitre de Justice d'après les manuscrits de la Mer Morte, et la litterature apocryphe rabbinique* (Avignon 1954).

26. *IQS* I, 1-11.

27. The Damascus Document distinguishes an "overseer" for each camp, and the "overseer of all the camps," and gives details regarding the age and qualifications of these officials and of the priests.

28. *IQS* I, 11-13.

29. *IQS* VI, 7-8.

30. The Damascus Document, however, contains legislation regarding the purity of offerings. Josephus says of the Essenes that they sent offerings to the Temple, but did not themselves offer sacrifice there, for, he wrote, "they offered their sacrifices themselves" (Ant. XVIII, i, 5) ; apparently, their ritual banquets took the place of the usual sacrificial meals. An interesting fragment from the second Qumran cave contains a kind of visionary description of a restored and perfected Temple and its cult, somewhat after the fashion of Ezechiel 40-48. Linked with other similar fragments, it suggests that the Qumran sect looked forward to a renewed partaking in the cult of the Temple in the new Jerusalem of the Messianic age. Cf. M. Baillet in *Rev. Bibl.* 62 (1955), pp. 222-245.

31. It is not expressly mentioned in the Rule, which, how-

ever, speaks of the obligation "no longer to walk in the pursuit of impure desires" (I, 6), and makes no mention anywhere of women and children, as does the Damascus Document, which permits marriage. However, in the cemetery of Qumran, skeletons identified as being of women were unearthed in certain of the graves. It might be that this represented an earlier stage in the sect's history (the cemetery being in use over a hundred years) or, better, that the women in question were pious strangers who had expressed a wish to be buried in this hallowed ground—parallel instances might be cited for Christian monastic settlements of later days.

32. In the Damascus Document, possession of one's goods and salary is allowed, except that a proportion of the latter must be handed over each month to the overseer. An interesting sidelight on community of property at Qumran is the fact that while coins in plenty were found in the main building, none at all were met with in the various caves outside.

33. *IQS* V, 1-10.

34. In the Damascus Document, the procedure of initiation is much simpler. The candidate simply presented himself to the "overseer of the camp," was examined, and then took the Oath of the Alliance, binding both himself and his children; in this engagement, some stress was also laid on the keeping of the calendar peculiar to the Sect and on Sabbath observance.

35. *CDC* I, 14-VI, 2.

36. Cf. J. P. Audet: "Affinités littéraires et doctrinales du Manuel de Discipline," *Rev. Bibl.* 60 (1952), pp. 219-238; 61 (1953), pp. 41-82.

37. *IQS* III, 15-19.

38. *IQS* III, 20-21.

39. *IQS* IV, 23-26.

40. Eternal life is referred to under a variety of expressions; wisdom of life, knowledge of eternity, eternal life, eternal hap-

piness, eternal destiny. There is no express mention of Resurrection of the Body. Did they deny this, as Josephus says of the Essenes (*Bell. Jud.* II, viii, 11) ? Yet other texts speak of God "purifying" the whole man, "removing all spirit of iniquity from his garments of flesh" etc. (*IQS* IV, 20-22) ; Vermès suggests by way of hypothesis the solution that they expected the Judgment to come within their own generation, and hence that the whole man would be directly taken up into glory (op. cit., p. 122). No certainty is possible at this stage, however.

41. On these Messianic expectations of the sect—very much confounded with the Judgment and End of the World—see J. T. Milik in *Rev. Bibl.* 60 (1953), pp. 290-2, and above, note 30.

42. "Les Documents du Désert de Juda et les Origines du Christianisme" *Anal. Lovan. Bibl. et Orient.*, II, 41, 1953, p. 26.

NOTES ON CHAPTER TWO

1. *Kommentar zum Neuen Testament aus Talmud und Midrasch* (4 vols., 1922-8).

2. This is true especially of the *Testament of the Twelve Patriarchs* and of *Henoch*. The influence of *Jubilees* and the *Testaments* on the Qumran documents and especially the Damascus Document is also incontestable: cf. J. T. Milik, in *Rev. Bibl.* 62 (1955), pp. 297-98 and F. M. Braun, ibid., pp. 5-6, note.

3. Between the *Testaments* and the Joannine literature, the following verbal likenesses have been noted: concepts of light and darkness, of truth and lying, "eternal life," "true judgment," "living water," "spirit of truth"; cf. E. Stauffer, *Die*

Theologie des Neuen Testaments, pp. 318-21 (Stuttgart, 1947), cited by Braun, loc. cit.

4. This is the method adopted by Coppens in his brief but excellent survey, *Les Documents du Désert de Juda et les Origines du Christianisme (Anal. Lovan. Bibl. Orient.,* ser. II, fasc. 41, 1953). It may be of interest here to note the points of contact between Qumran and the New Testament drawn up by Professor W. Baumgartner, an independent scholar of considerable standing. Among the resemblances he lists: esteem for the Old Testament and "midrashic interpretation"; condemnation of divorce; elaborate lists of sins; instructions for fraternal correction; community of property; doctrine of a suffering Messiah; rites of Baptism and Sacred Repast; sense of separation from the world; dualism (esp. St. John and St. Paul); spiritual cult; two characteristic expressions, "body of flesh" and "flesh of sin." Among the differences he notes the following aspects of the Qumran sect: preponderant role of priests and levites; effaced role of women and children; excessive legalism; charity restricted to members of the sect. A final difference lies in the all-important Christian teaching on the person of Jesus. ("Die Bedeutung der Höhlenfunde aus Palästina fur die Theologie," *Schweiz. Theol. Rundschau* XXIV (1954), pp. 49-63; summarized by J. Coppens, *Eph. Theol. Lov.* XXX (1954), pp. 533-4).

5. *The Dead Sea Scrolls* (Eng. trans., 1952), p. 99. See also S. E. Johnson: "The Dead Sea Manual of Discipline and the Jerusalem Church of Acts" in *Zeit. Alt. Wiss.* LXVI (1954), pp. 106-20.

6. *The Dead Sea Scrolls,* p. 46.

7. Op. cit., p. 29.

8. The Essenes, so Josephus and Philo tell us, were known to travel about Palestine, and colonies existed in various places.

9. Cf. *CDC* XIV, 12 ff.

10. Cf. Vermès: *Les Manuscrits du désert de Juda*, pp. 53-57. It is a question of small groups or cliques known as *Haburoth*. Chiefly preoccupied with the quest for greater ritual purity, their numbers met together for a kind of sacred meal, after the pattern of the Passover meal and the priestly meals in the Temple.

11. *IQS* III, 4.

12. *IQS* IV, 20-22 and III, 6-12.

13. *CDC* XIII, 7-10.

14. When the Damascus Document speaks of the "Overseer of all the Camps" as "master of all human secrets and of all the languages according to their number" (XIV, 9-10), the reference is probably to his skill in Biblical exegesis. Cf. R. North "The Damascus of Qumran Geography," *Pal. Expl. Quart.* LXXXVI (1955), p. 38.

15. Cf. Is. 58:6; 61:1 and 40:11. Ezech. 34:12 and Ps. 103:13.

16. *CDC* XIV, 9-10. Members of the judicial tribunal retired at the age of sixty (ibid., 4-10).

17. *IQS* IX, 21-22.

18. *IQS* VIII, 4-10; IX, 6, 9. *CDC* (B) XIX, 33-XX, 1.

19. Other resemblances with the scrolls in this passage (1 Pet. 2:4-10) are the antithesis of light and darkness, and the "stone rejected" and "living stones," cf. E. Lohse: "Paranese und Kerygma in 1 Petrusbrief," *Zeit. Neut. Wiss.* XLIV (1954), pp. 68-89.

20. Cf. 1 Tim. 3:15; Heb. 3:6; 1 Pet. 2:5 and 4:17 (House of God); Eph. 2:21 (Temple).

21. "Elect" (*CDC* IV, 3-4); "His Elect" (*IQpHab* IX, 12); "The Elect of grace" (*IQS* VIII, 6), "Congregation of His Elect" (*Comm. on Ps.* 37, I, 5; II, 5 and 16, etc.—published in *Pal. Expl. Quart.* LXXXVI (1954), pp. 69-75).

22. Rom. 8:33; Col. 3:12; 2 Tim. 2:10.

23. *CDC* (B), XX, 2; *IQS* V, 12, 18; VI, 20; IX, 12; *Comm. on Ps.* 37, II, 7, 8, 11.

24. Cf. Acts. 9:13 and 26:10; Rom. 15:25-6 and 31.

25. Exod. 22:31; Lev. 11:44; Deut. 7:6; 14:2, 21.

26. On *diatheke* as the equivalent of the Hebrew *berith*, with the sense of "alliance" see the series of articles entitled "Diatheke, Foedus an Testamentum?" by L. G. da Fonseca in *Bibl.*, vols. VIII-IX (1927-8).

27. *CDC* VI, 19:VIII, 21 and (B) XX, 12; *IQpHab* II, 3.

28. 2 Cor. 3:6; Heb. 7:22; 8:6 and 9:15; Luke 22:20 and 1 Cor. 11:25.

29. *IQS* I, 21-II, 18.

30. *IQH* IV, 30-33.

31. *IQS* X, 11-12; XI, 10-22.

32. Op. cit., p. 122.

33. Op. cit., p. 69.

34. Ps. 22:1; 41:2; 16:15; 72:25-6; 83:11.

35. The sectaries did not "bind heavy and insupportable burdens on others" while refusing to touch them themselves (Matt. 23:4); nor did they do all their works to be seen by men (ibid., 5); they did not "love the first places"—each had his own irrevocably determined place in the assembly (6); they did not "devour the houses of widows" (14), nor indulge in much oath-taking (16 ff.), they did not simply "clean the outside of the cup" (25) etc.

36. Op. cit., p. 31.

37. *IQS* I, 5; VII, 3-4; X, 24.

38. *IQS* I, 9; *CDC* VI, 20-21; *IQS* V, 20-VI, 1.

39. *CDC* VII, 2; *IQS* V, 24-25.

40. VII, 9-VIII, 1; (B) XIX, 34 ff.

41. Matt. 5:44; 28:19; 1 Tim. 2:1-6.

107

42. *CDC* XV, 7; XVII, 12; *IQS* I, 6; VIII, 13 ff. VII, 6; IX, 3-5.

43. *IQpHab* VIII, 1-2; *Comm. on Ps.* 37, I, 9.

44. *IQS* III, 7-9; IV, 20-23. Here we may note the occurrence of the expression "body of flesh," used in *IQpHab* IX, 2 in connexion with the providential punishment inflicted on the "Wicked Priest." It is also found in Col. 2:11; "in which ye are circumcised with a circumcision not made by hand, in the stripping of the body of the flesh." In St. Paul the expression is pregnant with the mortal antithesis between flesh and spirit; in the Habacuc Commentary it seems to be used in a merely physical sense. In any case, the expression is found already in Ecclus. 23:16 (Greek text). The parallel alleged between the cleansing of the "flesh" or "garments of flesh" (*IQS* III, 20 and IV, 20-21) and such passages as Rom. 8:3 and 2 Cor. 7:1 is somewhat remote.

45. *IQS* III, 22; *IQpHab* passim; *IQS* I, 13; VIII, 2.

46. *IQpHab* VII, 10; *IQS* IV, 5-6; *IQpHab* VII, 11-12; VIII, 2.

47. *IQS* II, 24-25; IV, 3.

48. *IQpHab* XII, 3, 6, 10; XII, 4. Cf. *IQH* II, 34; III, 25.

49. John 14:6; 2 Cor. 11:10; Gal. 2:5.

50. John 15:26; 16:13.

51. Matt. 19:13-14; 1 Cor. 4:13; Matt. 20:28 and 11:29.

52. Cf. especially Ps. 50:9 and 12.

NOTES ON CHAPTER THREE

1. Cp. *IQS* IX, 18; *CDC* III, 12; *IQS* I, 13-15.
2. *IQM* IX, 15 ff.; XVII, 6-7.

3. *CDC* V, 18-19; *IQS* III, 20 ff.

4. Cp. *IQH* III, 21-22 ("eternal assembly, army of saints, assembly of the sons of God") ; X, 8-11.

5. Cp. *IQS* III, 20 ff.

6. *CDC* IV, 12-18.

7. *IQM* XVIII, 1 ff.

8. *IQH* II, 26; IV, 12.

9. *IQH* III, 17-18.

10. Cp. Heinisch: *Theology of the Old Testament,* pp. 128-140 (Eng. trans. by W. G. Heidt, Minnesota, 1950).

11. Parallels from the apocrypha are cited by Heinisch (op. cit.) and Vermès (op. cit.) in the course of his commentary on the Qumran writings. Contrariwise, we find no parallel in the Qumran scrolls for such distinctively Christian applications as the doctrine of Guardian Angels (Matt. 18:10), the inferiority of the angels to Christ (Colossians and Ephesians, passim), and the idea that the just, at the Resurrection of the Body, are like "the angels in heaven" in purity (Mark 12:25).

12. Cp. Heinisch, op. cit., pp. 255-268, and E. Sutcliffe: *The Old Testament and the Future Life* (London, 1946).

13. M. Delcor: "L'eschatologie des documents de Khirbet Qumran," *Rech. Sc. Rel.* XXVI (1952), p. 386. It is interesting to note that the same author suggests the possibility of influence of the "Manual of Discipline" on the Book of Wisdom; cp. "L'immortalité de l'ame dans le livre de la Sagesse et dans les documents de Qumran," *Nouv. Rev. Theol.* LXXVI (1955), pp. 614-630; esp. p. 630. Cp. also A. M. Dubarle: "Une source du livre de la Sagesse?" *Rev. Sc. Phil. et Theol.* XXXVII (1953), pp. 425-443.

14. *IQS* II, 8; IV, 12-14; *IQpHab* V, 4.

15. Speaking of the just at the Last Day, the Rule says: "by the Spirit of God all his iniquities will be expiated so that he may contemplate the light of life" (*IQS* III, 6-7). The "man

109

of sin" is compared to the "man of lying," in *IQpHab* X, 9 ff., probably to be identified with the "Wicked Priest," sworn adversary of the Teacher of Righteousness. In a fragment from *IQ* (published in *Rev. Bibl.* 57 (1949), pl. XVII), which treats of the "Victory of Justice over Impiety," we read, "When justice, like the sun, dispels impiety like darkness, all those who leaned on the mysteries of iniquity will be no more" (line 6). Cp. Vermès, op. cit., p. 199.

16. See the full survey of Sutcliffe, op. cit., pp. 159-190.

17. John 16:11; cp. 12:3.

18. Op. cit., p. 35.

19. *IQS* VIII, 6; II, 29; III, 12; *IQH* III, 23; *IQS* IX, 3-4; II, 3-4; I, 27.

20. *IQS* IV, 2-8. Cp. Coppens, op. cit., pp. 36-37.

21. 1 Tim. 2:4.

22. Op. cit., p. 39, n. 53.

23. John 1:4-5; 3:19; 8:12.

24. Ibid., 12:35-36.

25. 1 John 4:1-6.

26. E.g. Braun, Grossouw, and to some extent Coppens.

27. Coppens suggests that, among the Jewish converts in the early churches of Jerusalem and Judea, there may have been some of the sectaries (op. cit., pp. 28-29). Braun has a series of theories to account for apparent contacts with various portions of the New Testament. For the Acts and St. Paul's Captivity Epistles, he suggests that there were converts from Qumran among the "crowd of priests that obeyed the Law" (Acts 6:7), who were subsequently scattered by persecution to Phoenicia, Cyprus, Antioch and Ephesus, where St. Paul may have met them. After the destruction of Qumran in A.D. 68, the sectaries may have settled in Syria, and it is possible that St. John may have adapted his writings somewhat (as regards

vocabulary) with a view to winning them over. Even before this, the Baptist seems to have given an initial impetus, since his spirit and vocabulary were of the Essenian type, and Jesus, too, may have had intermittent relations with members of the sect in Judea. Apollos—whom Braun accepts as the writer of Hebrews—may also have contacted the sectaries. (Cp. "L'arrière-fond judaique du quatrième évangile et la Communauté de l'Alliance," *Rev. Bibl.* 62 (1955), pp. 5-44.) W. Grossouw suggests that St. Paul made contact with the sectaries established at Damascus during his three-year sojourn in Syria after his conversion (Gal. 1:17). (Cp. "The Dead Sea Scrolls and the New Testament," *Stud. Cath.* XXVII (1953), p. 5.) Syrian contacts, in the case of the Fourth Gospel (whose Joannine origin is rejected), are also postulated by L. Mowry in "The Dead Sea Scrolls and the Gospel of John," *Bib. Arch.* XVII (1954), pp. 78-97. These last two theories labour to some extent from the defect of taking the "Damascus" of *CDC* in a literal, as distinct from a symbolic, sense. On this matter see the excellent treatment of R. North, "The Damascus of Qumran Geography," *Pal. Expl. Quart.* LXXXVI (1955), pp. 34-48.

28. E.g. 2 Sam. 2:7; 1 Sam. 20:1 and 25:17.

29. John 14:6.

30. *CDC* VII, 3-4; V, 11; *IQS* III, 7.

31. *CDC* II, 12; *IQS* IV, 21.

32. Cp. Heinisch, op. cit., pp. 116-123.

33. *The Dead Sea Scrolls; a preliminary survey,* esp. pp. 64-65. It should be noted that parallel texts in the Rule suggest that the phrase "Unique Master" of *CDC* XX, 1 is due to a medieval scribal alteration, which read "yahid" (unique) for "yahad" (Community). Thus Vermès renders "Master of the Community" (op. cit., p. 171).

34. Op. cit., pp. 96 and 99.

35, 36. It is simply a question of the "taking away" of the Teacher of Righteousness (cp. *CDC* XIX, 33), which does not necessarily connote a violent death. The text which refers to the Wicked Priest's persecution of the Teacher, and upon which Dupont-Sommer leaned rather heavily in his earlier work, does not—according to the rendering which even he now accepts—contain any clear reference to death or even torture: "Its explanation concerns the Wicked Priest who set out to pursue the Teacher of Righteousness in order to lead him astray, in the passion of his fury, on the place of his exile" (*IQpHab* XI, 4-6; cp. Vermès, op. cit., p. 133).

37. Op. cit., p. 65.

38. Cp. *supra*, p. 25.

39. The Qumran writings avoid the Davidic titles in reference to the Messiah; in fact, in *CDC* the prophecies referring to the Davidic Messiah are interpreted allegorically. In a fragment of 4*Q*—a kind of "book of Messianic testimonies"—the Messianic prophecies assembled refer to the "prophet" of Deut. 18:18, the "Star" of Balaam's oracle (Num. 24:15-17) and the blessing of Levi (Deut. 33:8-11). Cp. J. T. Milik in *Rev. Bibl.* 60 (1953), pp. 290-292.

40. Theories of K. Holl, Harnack and R. Bultmann respectively (Coppens, op. cit., p. 34).

41. *CDC* VI, 15-16 and XVI, 14-15 (Qorban); *CDC* XI, 13-14 (prohibition of drawing one's beast out of the well on the Sabbath).

42. Cp. C. H. Hunzinger: "Neues Licht auf Lc 2, 14," *Zeit. Neut. Wiss.* XLIV (1952-3), pp. 84-90. The author thinks that the Qumran vocabulary (referring to the sectaries as being God's chosen ones) confirms the existence of some current Semitic equivalent for *eudokia* ("good will") in the sense of *God's* good pleasure and beneficence.

43. We have seen above how Braun suggests sporadic contact between Jesus and the sectaries in Judea. In a recent article on the Qumran excavations, G. Lankester Harding suggests that Jesus may have visited Qumran, and that the Baptist very probably went there (*Ill. London News*, Sept. 3rd, 1955). There is no suggestion of this in the gospels; in fact, I think that the character and very closed nature of the sect, and the relations of both John and Jesus with official orthodox Judaism seem to render it unlikely.

44. Op. cit., p. 39. A little above, he writes, "It is possible, as Martin noted formerly with regard to the book of Henoch, that the Qumran sect played its part in publicizing, among Jewish circles won over to pietist and apocalyptic ideas, a certain number of beliefs which prepared the ground for the advent of Christianity, and which are found occasionally, in whole or in part, in Christian vocabulary or teaching."

NOTE: This chapter was completed before the present writer had access to the article of R. E. Brown, "The Qumran Scrolls and the Joannine Gospel and Epistles" (*Cath. Bibl. Quart.* XVII (1955), pp. 403-419), which arose out of a paper given in the course of a seminar on the Dead Sea Scrolls conducted at Johns Hopkins University by Professor Albright. In this article, under various heads, the author studies "the similarities and differences that exist between the modified dualistic concept of light and darkness in the Qumran literature and the Joannine literature" (p. 418). "It should be evident," he concludes, "that the basic difference between the two theologies is Christ" (ibid.). As regards the question of dependence of St. John upon the Qumran writings, the author, in a subsequent article (ibid., pp. 559-574), believes that he may have had a general acquaintance—rather than direct contacts—with Qumran thought and expression, possibly *via* John the Baptist. Both this author and L. Mowry (see note above) had access to the MSS. of Prof. Albright's forthcoming study, entitled "Recent discoveries in Palestine and the Gospel of John" which will be published in the *Festschrift* for C. H. Dodd.

NOTES ON CHAPTER FOUR

1. *The Scrolls from the Dead Sea* (New York and London [W. H. Allen], 1955). References throughout are to the American edition, published by Oxford University Press.

2. Cp. pp. 100-102.

3. E.g. "let not yourselves be called masters . . ." (Matt. 23:10) and the humility of the sectaries, especially their officers; the "fountain of living water" (John 4:14) and the "well of living water" of the Zadokite Document; "all things were made through him, and without him was made nothing that was made" (John 1:2-3) and "by his knowledge everything has been brought into being. And everything that is, he established by his purpose; and apart from him, nothing is done" (*IQS* XI, 11); cp. pp. 37, 71, 95. Apropos of the last example, need we note that the subject of the Joannine text is the Word of God who became incarnate, a doctrine wanting in the Qumran texts, which simply echo the thoughts of the Psalms, etc., on the creative power of the one God of the Old Law?

4. Op. cit., pp. 70, 92, 87.

5. Op. cit., p. 94.

6. Ibid.

7. Op. cit., p. 93.

8. Op. cit., p. 94.

9. Op. cit., pp. 92-93.

10. Op. cit., p. 40.

11. Op. cit., p. 97.

12. Op. cit., pp. 95-96.

13. Op. cit., p. 96.

14. Op. cit., p. 95. The allusion is to the text, "I am not come to bring peace, but a sword" (Matt. 10:34).

15. Op. cit., p. 97.

16. Op. cit., pp. 97-98.

17. Op. cit., p. 108.

18. Op. cit., p. 98. True, on the same page, Wilson does pay tribute to the "acute and exhaustive study," the "keenness and coolness that seem quite objective" of church scholars; nonetheless, "one feels a certain nervousness, a reluctance to take hold of the subject and place it in historical perspective."

19. Op. cit., p. 101.

20. Cp. *IQS* IV, 23-26; *CDC* VII, 9-VIII, 1; XIX, 34 ff.

21. Cp. M. De Jonge: *The Testaments of the Twelve Patriarchs* (Assen, 1953) and J. T. Milik in *Rev. Bibl.* 62 (1955), pp. 297-298 and 398-406. The *Testament of Levi,* though now incorporated in the *Testaments,* is a distinct and pre-Christian work; fragments in Aramaic were found in the Cairo Geniza, and portions of three MSS. in the fourth Qumran cave, besides a minute fragment from Cave One.

22. "Le Testament de Lévi en Araméen," *Rev. Bibl.* 62 (1955), p. 405.

23. *IQS* VIII, 23.

24. *IQS* IX, 21-22.

25. *IQS* VII, 18 ff.; 23. *CDC* XIX, 35-XX, 1.

26. *IQS* VII, 24-25.

27. Matt. 2:23; Luke 2:51; cp. 4:16.

28. Mark 1:9.

29. Mark 6:1-3.

30. John 6:42.

31. Ibid., 43-47.

32. John 7:15; cp. v. 27 "We know this man, where he is from."

33. Ibid., 16.

34. Cp. 4:34; 5:19; 7:28; 15:15. Cp. the recurring phrase "I am come . . ." used in all four gospels in connection with the preaching, miracles and redemptive death of Jesus.

35. This same "argument from silence" might be extended to cover the whole question of direct contact and borrowings between the New Testament and the Scrolls. The gospels bring us into contact with all the various religious and political parties among the Jews—Sadducees and Priests, Pharisees and Scribes, Herodians and disciples of the Baptist; in them we meet a generous cross-section of Palestinian society—the rich, the "princes of the people," the Sanhedrin, together with the despised publicans, the public sinners, the lepers, the poor, women and children; we meet the Roman centurion, the Greeks in the Temple, the Hellenized court of Herod, the Canaanite Woman. Elsewhere in the New Testament, we read of various false "Messiahs," a Galilean and an Egyptian, of members of the priestly family, of Romans and Greeks with their various philosophical sects, of the Baptist's disciples again, etc. Not a word about the Qumran sect! Of course, an argument from silence can be pressed too far; but, at all events, it seems that the *onus probandi* must rest very much with those who claim direct contacts between the Qumran sect and the early Christians.

36. Cp. Lankester Harding in the *Illustrated London News*, 3rd Sept., 1955: "John the Baptist was almost certainly an Essene: he undoubtedly derived the idea of ritual baptism or immersion from them" (p. 379).

37. John 1:24-25.

38. Luke 1:17 and 15.

39. Luke 1:76.

40. Ibid., 80.

41. Matt. 3:7-10; Luke 3:10-14.

42. "Do penance, for the Kingdom of heaven is at hand" (Matt. 3:2).

43. Matt. 3:11.

44. Luke 3:3; cp. Matt. 3:6: the people came to be baptized "confessing their sins."

45. John 1:25.

46. John 4:1-2. We may note, too, the Pharisees' own predilection for ritual ablutions of all kinds, of their persons and of what they used; cp. Mark 7:3-4.

47. Mark 12:30.

48. Op. cit., p. 98.